Loretta Spencer
A Passion for Service

A Candid Memoir
by the First Woman Mayor
of Huntsville, Alabama

Loretta Spencer
A Passion for Service

A Candid Memoir
by the First Woman Mayor
of Huntsville, Alabama

Fresh Ink Group
Guntersville

Loretta Spencer, A Passion for Service
A Candid Memoir by the First Woman Mayor of Huntsville, Alabama

Fresh Ink Group
An Imprint of:
The Fresh Ink Group, LLC
1021 Blount Avenue #931
Guntersville, AL 35976
Email: info@FreshInkGroup.com
FreshInkGroup.com

Edition 1.0 2024

Editing by Ann Marie Martin
Cover design by Stephen Geez / FIG
Book design by Amit Dey / FIG
Associate publisher Beem Weeks / FIG

Cataloging-in-Publication Recommendations:
BIO010000 BIOGRAPHY & AUTOBIOGRAPHY / Political
BIO022000 BIOGRAPHY & AUTOBIOGRAPHY / Women
POL052000 POLITICAL SCIENCE / Women in Politics

Library of Congress Control Number: 2024916882

ISBN-13: 978-1-964998-08-4 Softcover
ISBN-13: 978-1-964998-09-1 Hardcover
ISBN-13: 978-1-964998-10-7 Ebooks

Acknowledgements

Thank you to everyone who helped bring this project together: Blake Hudson, City Videographer; staff writer Denise Taylor; final editor Ann Marie Martin; my publisher at Fresh Ink Group, Stephen Geez; and of course my son, J Spencer, for help with the photos, editing, and everything else.

Contents

Chapter One

Welcome to Huntsville!

*L*oretta Spencer understands the power of good roads.
They're vital to a city's quality of life, enabling residents to move easily from home to work, school, shopping, recreation, and more. They're our municipal circulatory system, our city's life blood. And if the roads are good enough – especially those arteries that bring visitors into the city – they can become an important route to the city's future growth and prosperity.

That's why, on Oct. 10, 1996, newly installed Huntsville Mayor Loretta Spencer spent much of her first day on the job leading a team to pick up trash on Memorial Parkway. She assembled a broad coalition of 50 garden club members from across the city along with other volunteers, all the city's department directors, and 75 work-release inmates. They started north of Alabama A&M University at the Mount Charron neighborhood and worked south to Redstone Road, not far from the Tennessee River. She still keeps the reflective vest she wore in her car.

Improving city beautification and maintenance was one of Spencer's stated priorities during the mayoral campaign. Yes, she wanted to create a more appealing place for residents to live, but a larger goal lay beyond the city's limits. She thought about out-of-towners traveling into Huntsville – representatives of international high-tech corporations or a famous hotel chain or a popular retailer – people who typically would arrive, look around, and leave town unannounced. She imagined their first views of Huntsville, and she determined to create the best possible first impressions.

"How can you ask a company to invest in your city if the city doesn't invest in itself?" she pointed out during the campaign.

Top: Dave Dieter/Huntsville Times
Right: Glenn Baeske/Huntsville Times

At top, Loretta Spencer takes the oath of office from Judge Lynwood Smith. Spencer is the first woman to head any of the state's four largest cities. At right, Spencer and other volunteers pick up trash today along the median of Memorial Parkway north of Mastin Lake Road.

October 1996

This clipping from The Huntsville Times shows Mayor Loretta Spencer fulfilling her campaign promise to clean up Memorial Parkway on her first day in office.

From beautification, she mapped out a figurative road to her other top goals for the city: A well-maintained city attracts new retailers and businesses and jobs. Those new employers enhance and diversify the city's tax base, which funds improvements to the school system to improve the quality of education for all Huntsville students. Better employment opportunities and better schools lead to more and happier residents. And the road to a brighter tomorrow goes on from there.

Politicians – especially those running for a new office, be it city, state, or national – like to campaign on their intentions to clean up corruption, waste, or inefficiency. But to literally clean up one of the city's major traffic arteries? That's rare – perhaps even a first. Certainly no one could recall it happening in Huntsville.

Establishing a new "first" was not unusual for Spencer. It was the latest in a long series. After coming in first in a crowded municipal election and then easily winning a runoff, she had been elected as the first female mayor of one of Alabama's four largest cities. That alone had already given another historic "first" to Huntsville, home to Alabama's first constitution and America's first moon rocket.

However, Spencer began achieving significant "firsts" long before she made it to City Hall.

In 1970, she became the first woman named to the board of directors of the Boys Club, the youth civic association that later became the Boys & Girls Club. One of the men on the board said he didn't think she was qualified for the position. She showed him, doing such a good job that he was the person who nominated her for a second term.

Boys Club Boost

A raffle of a TV set by the Acme Club has netted $3,500 for the Boys Club on Abbingdon Avenue. Presenting the check Thursday was Acme Club president Allen Brinkley, right. Accepting from left, were Boys Club treasurer Gig Robinson president Loretta Spencer and Board member Harrison McMains III. (News Staff Phot   David Phillips)

Loretta Spencer's organizational abilities and hard work quickly showed doubters that she was more than up to the task of serving on the board of the Boys Club, which later became the Boys & Girls Club.

She became the first woman on the Huntsville Planning Commission in 1977 when Mayor Joe Davis asked her to serve. She chaired the Planning Commission from 1981 through 1989 and was involved in the further development of Cummings Research Park (CRP) with the addition of CRP West.

To achieve success with each of these entities – as well as many more civic and nonprofit groups around town, including the Von Braun Civic Center and the Huntsville Botanical Garden – Spencer relied on establishing strong personal relationships and paying close attention to details. The people she worked with expected her to go on to be a successful mayor because they'd seen her organizational ability and talent for bringing people together for a common goal. They also knew she possessed the optimism, enthusiasm, and tenacity necessary to ignite Huntsville's economic development.

Many factors contributed to Loretta Spencer becoming a capable volunteer worker, civic leader, and elected official: She grew up in Huntsville – her family moved from Birmingham when she was 7 – and early influences from family and friends formed a strong sense of community. After college, she taught elementary school and then married and raised a family while working to make their hometown a better place to live. This biography chronicles these experiences and shows their impact on her mayoral decisions and initiatives as well as the challenges she faced.

During Mayor Spencer's tenure in office, October 1996 to November 2008, she set Huntsville on the road to where it is today in 2024: the largest city in Alabama. Her administration's plans, policies, and relationships brought to fruition or planted the seeds of many of the shopping, dining, sporting, and other entertainment options enjoyed by current residents and visitors. Much of the robust tax base that funds these options grew from employment opportunities that she helped nurture – from Base Realignment and Closure additions to Redstone Arsenal to Toyota Motor Manufacturing and lots more in between. Many of the major construction projects springing up all over town have roots in her administration, too.

Welcome to the life and times of Loretta Purdy Spencer – a collection of stories and snapshots from Huntsville, Alabama.

Chapter Two

A Foundation for Community Service

*L*oretta Spencer's strong family and community ties formed the firm foundation of her dedication to public service, first as civic volunteer and then as Huntsville's mayor. She learned many valuable lessons growing up that would fuel her later success.

Loretta Lee Purdy was born on June 20, 1937, in Birmingham, Alabama, the first child of John and Sarah Purdy. Her father was in the mortuary business, and her mother was a homemaker. Brother John arrived in 1938. Sister Patricia Ann joined the family in 1944 after they moved to Huntsville. Loretta always called her sister "Doll."

"My brother and I always loved to wait for Daddy to come home from work," Loretta recalls of her early years when they were still living in Birmingham.

Some of those memories include circumstances brought on by World War II.

"They checked the blocks because the war was on, and we would have air raid drills. One night, John and I were in the bathtub, and mother was bathing us. I think we had a little flashlight because we couldn't see any light through any windows, and the shades were pulled. She was trying to hurry because you weren't necessarily notified ahead of time. We could hear a man hollering, 'All the lights out!'"

Loretta still has a copy of the ration booklet her mother used to get sugar and other staples during the war.

Loretta Purdy at about age 7.

"The reason Daddy was not activated," she said, "was because they wanted people who worked in funeral homes to stay because they had to bury the ones who were killed during the war."

In 1944, when Loretta was 7, her father was asked to move to Huntsville to manage Laughlin Service Funeral Home, serving the community since 1868.

"The funeral home was downtown, and the building still exists to this day. It had the most gorgeous stained glass windows in it," she recalls. "Some of them were taken out when we were building a new location, where it is now on Bob Wallace, in 1958 when I was in college."

When the Purdys moved to town, Huntsville's population was about 10,000, a big change from Birmingham's 267,583, as recorded by the 1940 Census.

"Daddy went ahead of us and got settled down, and he looked around at what was available."

Loretta's parents, John and Sarah Purdy, stand in front of the family home on Surrey Road in Huntsville, circa 1944.

Mr. Purdy found a house on Surrey Road off Whitesburg Drive. Today the neighborhood is in the central part of Huntsville. In 1944 it was almost in the county. The city limits extended to present-day Drake Avenue and Whitesburg Drive. At that time Whitesburg was a tar and gravel road, very different from the asphalt of today and not good for roller skating. The children used the smoother driveways of neighbors for this popular pastime.

There was no direct road from Birmingham to Huntsville in 1944. The Tennessee River bridge on U.S. 231 had not yet been built. So, whenever Loretta and her mother and brother came to Huntsville, they took a train from Birmingham to Decatur, where her father picked them up. Decatur, population 16,604 in the 1940 Census, was larger and had brighter prospects for growth at that time than Huntsville.

Despite falling short for roller skating, Whitesburg Drive was one of Huntsville's better roads in 1944. Most of the other roads in town and the surrounding area, which was predominantly farmland, were gravel roads with no tar. That meant dusty vehicles. Loretta's father liked to joke with Carl Jones about the long, dusty drive out to the Jones farm whenever the family or children visited.

"My dad had to keep a clean car all the time because he was driving the families to the funerals and to the cemetery," Loretta said. "Whenever he would see Mr. Carl, he'd say, 'When you going to pave this?' He always went the extra mile and felt that the car should be clean to show respect to grieving families."

Jones Valley is in the central part of Huntsville today, but it was considered quite a distance away from the downtown area in the 1940s. Loretta recalls the farmers who helped shape Huntsville.

"I just remember those two men, Carl T. Jones and Walton Fleming. They were very much the leaders of Huntsville."

To Loretta, they were the well-respected fathers of her friends Betsy Jones and Gay and Sally Fleming.

"Mr. Carl was an engineer at G.W. Jones, and Walton Fleming had all that land across on the other side of the road called Piedmont. The farm people who worked for them had houses over across the road, and they farmed part of that land."

Loretta and John rode into town with their father on Saturdays when he drove to the funeral home. Loretta recalls fun times with her friends downtown as well as early lessons in budgeting a dollar.

"Gay's uncle was one of the managers of the downtown movie theater. She was always saying, 'Come on,' but my mama always insisted that we paid. We could go to the picture show – they called it the picture show in those days – for 10 cents. Johnny and I had our dollar-a-week allowance, and we could go for 50 cents: a dime for each of us for the admission and a nickel for a bag of popcorn. Then we could go to the Nuway on the square to get a hot dog and drink for lunch for that other quarter."

Loretta and brother John and their friends enjoyed going to the picture shows at the Lyric Theater in downtown Huntsville when they were growing up.

Loretta's ability to manage her money included a talent for convincing other people – mostly brother John – to join her plans.

"I always had something in the layaway at B.F. Goodrich on the corner from the Lyric Theater. I would talk my brother out of his 50 cents because we had pay on the layaway. Or he'd have to give me a quarter, and I'd put a quarter with it. The manager of the store had a child at the Fifth Avenue School, where we went to elementary school, and they knew our family and that I'd be good for it. Daddy was always telling me it was mother's birthday coming up or Mother's Day was coming up. I always was buying something and putting it on layaway.

"One of things I was most proud of I found at Kress Department Store next to the theater. I bought my mother a bottle of perfume out of part of my allowance when some anniversary or birthday was coming up. The bottle was navy blue glass, and I thought it was so pretty. It had a gold top."

Loretta learned to save her money and to be thoughtful of her parents.

"My daddy was always reminding us, 'Your mama works hard.' That was important, and everybody would agree with that because she was always at church and PTA. She had such a good reputation for her cooking. The schools would hold a cakewalk at the Halloween Carnival as a fundraiser, and they made a lot of money to buy books for the library. If they knew Mama baked it, the bidding was very good on her cakes."

Loretta loved Fifth Avenue School, which she attended from second through sixth grade. John started first grade there. She developed an early love of teaching. She would organize play Bible school sessions with neighborhood children in the family garage with herself as the teacher.

Loretta recalls a wonderful childhood growing up in Huntsville. They enjoyed summertime parades, complete with musical instruments, marching around neighborhood streets. Those instruments often included a single bugle owned by her brother and something they made into a drum as well as a baton from the fair that came to town.

"Kids had to be creative in those days," she said.

Sometimes the fun and games led to serious consequences as on the day that Loretta decided to teach the family dog a new trick. She had seen a dog walking over a barrel and thought it would be an easy trick to teach. To show her dog how to do it, she began walking over the barrel. Turns out, it was harder than it looked, and she fell.

There were few doctors in Huntsville, just family practitioners who would drive to homes to make house calls, but there was a clinic in the downtown area at the corner of Franklin Street and Gates Avenue. At the clinic, Loretta found out that she had broken her wrist in two places. As a left-hander, she remembers being thankful that it was her right arm.

Typical of small communities, neighbors in Huntsville helped each other and worked together on larger projects. When someone was sick or there was a death in a family, neighbors provided home-cooked food to those who needed it. Ladies were known for their special dishes which could be counted on to be part of meals provided.

Closeness was not just for trying times. Backyards were open. Families gathered between houses for shared meals, conversation and games to pass the time. People knew each other well, and their lives were connected in so many ways.

Loretta holds a special memory of making stops at the Van Valkenburg home. Margaret Ann Van Valkenburg lived in a beautiful antebellum home located next door to the funeral home. Whenever the children spotted Mrs. Van Valkenburg sitting on her front porch, they knew it was a signal for them to stop by and enjoy her cookies.

Going to Monte Sano for a family picnic was a treat, especially in the hot summer months. This was a time well before air conditioners were common in homes. Everyone had window fans in their houses. The temperature on Monte Sano was known to be usually about 10 degrees cooler than it was in the valley.

Daily activities for the children could span two blocks. There was one library downtown. A little recreation park, although not well kept up, was at the end of two streets. A popular spot to play ball was the large empty field behind their house with woods at the end of the field. Loretta was often found on the mound pitching left-handed. The wooded area had a sassafras tree which gave them the opportunity to make sassafras tea. Her mother had shown them how to make tea from the root bark of the tree.

Loretta and John both showed leadership skills early. She was the editor of the Huntsville High School newspaper, The Red & Blue, during her senior year. She also earned the distinction of Outstanding Senior, which was voted on by the teachers and presented by the American Legion each year. Faculty helped choose this honor, which was presented at graduation. John was also the Outstanding Senior his senior year, the year following Loretta.

During Loretta's high school years, important changes were happening in Huntsville that would set the city on a high trajectory.

"What was special about high school that was very important to me," Loretta remembers, "is in our 10th grade we had German children in the classroom with us. I remember Axel Roth, and he was so smart. He married a Huntsville girl in later times. He and I had science class together, and I beat him on a lab test one day, and that made me proud as everything."

The Red and Blue

THE YOUTH OF TODAY IS THE WORLD OF TOMORROW

VOL. 19—NO. 16   HUNTSVILLE HIGH SCHOOL   MAY 28, 1954

VOLUME NINETEEN IS DEDICATED TO MRS. ELIZABETH HOWELL

COMMENCEMENT SET FOR MAY 28

Seniors Look Forward To Graduation

On May 28, approximately one hundred seniors will march down the aisle to strains of "Pomp and Circumstances" to receive that piece of paper they spent twelve years working for—a diploma.

Commencement exercises will carry out the class theme, "The Youth of Today Is The World of Tomorrow."

The five commencement speakers will be Billy Hooper, class president; Don Atkinson, president of the Student Council; Ronald Mitchell, vice-president of the senior class; Patricia Stutts, valedictorian; and Sandra Stribling, salutatorian.

May 26 was the date for the annual Class Day program. A play, written by Jeanne Tyson and Jane Anderson was presented at 10:00. Speakers were Tracy Jackson, class lawyer; Jeanne Tyson, prophet; Dudley Hall Buchanan, poet; Alice Hinshaw, giftorian; and Betty Beamguard, historian.

Tri-Hi-Y Elect Officers

The National Honor Society and the Tri-Hi-Y recently met to elect officers for the next school year.

Sarah Cole was elected president of the Honor Society, while Patsy Stewart won the vote as vice-president, Janie Sue Craft is the new secretary, and Bob Gay will serve as treasurer.

The Tri-Hi-Y chose Sandra Kel-

Student Body Elects Canterbury As Council Pres.

Ball, Dickey, Frank Also Win Ballot

Henry Canterbury was recently elected as president of the Student Council for next year. Dwain Ball won the vote for vice-president; Ann Dickey, secretary-treasurer; and Butch Frank, sergeant-at-arms.

An assembly was held the day before the election and each candidate gave his campaign speech. Amid jokes and promises, the candidates managed to live through the rally and everyone anxiously awaited the outcome of the voting.

As the results of the first ballot were tabulated, it was found that a run-off between some of the candidates must be held. In the race for president, fighting Henry Canterbury won on the first ballot. Ann Dickey also won the office of secretary-treasurer

Working For The Deadline—Loretta Purdy (left), listens intently to the facts for a story while Sarah Cole (right), Marianne Searcy (back, left), and Dickie Watts (back, right), wait for instructions.

LORETTA PURDY TO EDIT VOLUME 20

Cole To Serve As Associate Editor; Searcy, Business Manager; Watts, Circulation Manager

Because of her outstanding qualities of leadership and dependability, Loretta Purdy has been chosen by a student-faculty committee as Editor-in-chief of the Twentieth Volume of the Red and Blue.

The May 28, 1954, issue of Huntsville High School's newspaper, The Red and Blue, announces Loretta Purdy's selection as editor-in-chief of the paper's 20th volume.

Many years later as mayor, Loretta would talk about the arrival of her German classmates and their families in Huntsville during an interview on CNN.

"They asked me how we got along with the German children. I said we got along fine. I said they were always so very smart. They moved into our city in 1949 and 1950, and I said that we should be thankful that we have these wonderful scientists coming to Huntsville, and they're going to keep Redstone Arsenal open. We thought that it was a blessing to have a commanding general at the base and then that they were all working so well together with Senator Sparkman and Milton Cummings."

Loretta recalls growing up with the daughters of Milton Cummings, a founder of Cummings Research Park.

"One of them was in my class, and one was in my brother's class. They were always good friends."

When U.S. Sen. John Sparkman, a Huntsville resident, helped to bring the German rocket scientists to Redstone Arsenal in 1950, Huntsville was still a cotton market town of 16,437. It had grown since Loretta and her family arrived, but not by much.

After graduating from Huntsville High School in 1955, Loretta went to college at The University of Alabama, graduating in 1959.

"When I graduated from college with a teacher's degree, my beautiful, wonderful second-grade teacher at Fifth Avenue School had become principal, and she could hire her own faculty. She called me up in June before I graduated in August."

A change in major resulted in Loretta graduating at the end of the summer instead of in May and led her to take a class that her father questioned.

"Because I was in pre-med for the first two years in college, I had to take two more courses. One was making a basket out of Popsicle sticks. I made a coffee table for my daddy, and he said, 'This is what I just paid $9,000 for?' Because that's what my education cost him. I had to do that and had to take history of education."

After graduation, she joined her parents on their usual summer vacation.

"We drove to Florida with that coffee table, and we met Mom and Daddy because Daddy always took the month of August for vacation. By then I'd had a little sister come along. She's seven and a half years younger than me. I would babysit her."

After that family vacation, Loretta returned to her beloved hometown and started teaching at Fifth Avenue School.

In the years that followed, she married and had two children, J and Sarah. She also found time to contribute to the community and city. Like her mother, she became known for her culinary skills, which served many city milestones well, but her contributions took paths well beyond bake sales and cookbooks.

*Some years after she graduated from The University of Alabama,
Loretta Spencer, center, walks arm-in-arm with Alabama Crimson
Tide head football coach Paul "Bear" Bryant.*

Chapter Three

Volunteering for a Better Community

*L*oretta Spencer had built a strong reputation as an effective community volunteer long before 1996, when she first ran for mayor of Huntsville and won. Some of her 11 opponents in that first race belittled her volunteer experience. Perhaps they didn't realize that volunteer organizations need the same high level of innovation, good management and hard work to succeed as any commercial business endeavor. Perhaps they were just grasping for anything to stop her. At any rate, they seriously underestimated the value of her experience.

From growing up in a close-knit family and community and then working to make that community a better place to live through volunteerism, she learned three valuable lessons:

1. Find out as much as you can about each situation.
2. Pay attention to details.
3. Never forget the personal touch.

"I built teams to have the best outcome for all the things that I had the opportunity to serve on," Loretta said, emphasizing the importance of good team members.

She smiles when talking about the many projects she worked on and the people she worked with as a volunteer and later as mayor.

"Everything is about relationships and people working together on the same page."

Loretta stresses the importance of bringing different personalities with varied strengths together to form stronger teams. Fostering a good team environment is always key to success, and her outgoing, inclusive personality and background gave her that ability.

The 1996 mayoral race wasn't the first time Loretta had to prove that she was more than qualified for a job. During the 1970s and 1980s, she served on several boards of directors that had been predominantly or exclusively male before she joined. Sometimes she had to win over a male skeptic.

When Loretta became the first female board member of the Boys Club, later the Boys & Girls Club, one of the male board members said that he didn't think she could do the job. She tackled that challenge in her typical fashion.

To prepare for each board meeting, she extensively researched all prospective projects and topics so she could provide intricate details and answer any questions. This helped the organization grow so it could serve more children in the community.

And the doubting male board member? She won him over. He even nominated her for a second term.

Other volunteer achievements came with different challenges.

Huntsville is a major medical hub today, but during the 1970s, the city needed more doctors, particularly specialists. For example, people who required dialysis had to drive to Birmingham or Nashville to see a nephrologist for treatment. The city was trying to bring a nephrologist to town, but he wouldn't come unless specialized equipment was provided.

Loretta was president of the Grace Club Auxiliary, now the Junior League, and she led the effort to raise money to purchase this expensive equipment. The club held several events to meet its goal. One of these was The Grace Club Auxiliary Follies, which Loretta chaired. It became a fundraising staple in the community for many years.

For the Follies, the club would hire a professional director through the Cargill Company to come to Huntsville for a three-week stay. He would create a theme, and they would hire an orchestra. Then they would hold auditions for couples. Husbands and wives would rehearse nightly for each act. The event was so popular within the community that it would sell out.

Along with the dialysis equipment, the event also funded the purchase of an audiometer to test the hearing of elementary students. At that time, the closest one of any quality was in Oklahoma, which made it difficult for people to access that level of diagnosis.

The Auxiliary also boosted the city's entertainment and tourism profile by purchasing a grand piano and furnishings for the Green Room at the Von Braun Civic Center (VBCC) for its opening in 1974.

A huge element of Follies success came from local businesses buying ads. Loretta knew that people would support businesses that invested in improving the quality of life in Huntsville, and she drove home that point to sell ads.

"Of course, we always thanked businesses that supported the events with a note. However, when the businesses gained customers, we knew it was a bit better than any thank-you note we would send."

Loretta became directly involved with the operations of the VBCC when she was appointed to its board in October 1976. This time, she was the second woman on the board, Martha Simms (later Martha Simms Rambo) being the first.

The VBCC facility became the core of large entertainment events which enhanced the quality of life in Huntsville. The board knew that if it was successful, it would set the stage in the future for regional meetings which would then lead to larger conferences selecting Huntsville as a destination.

But the new facility wasn't ready to handle that bright future. In its first three years, the VBCC offered only a catering kitchen. Large event meals had to come from a restaurant at the airport, and the hot boxes could not consistently keep the food warm on the journey.

The VBCC needed a commercial kitchen to reach its potential. In regard to catering, Loretta told the board that "they needed to either get into the business or get out of it."

When they added a suitable kitchen, the first luncheon was for the Kappa Delta Sorority Alum Conference, and the stakes were high. If the event was a success, word would spread, and other organizations would want to hold large events at the VBCC. If it was a failure, it would be harder to get future business.

The Kappa Delta conference was a success, and the board realized that they needed a good chef to meet forecasted growth.

During the VBCC's early years, the arena was not consistently rented and provided only periodic income, so the revenue from meals served at chamber banquets, conferences and conventions was vital to the facility's operations. The opening of the North Hall in 1989 improved the financial situation as it quickly became the most used venue for large luncheons and dinners.

Joe Davis, mayor of Huntsville from 1968 to 1988, was determined that the VBCC would include an arena to accommodate large crowds for a variety of events. An arena was not in the original plan for the facility, but it quickly showed its benefit to the community. People came to Huntsville from surrounding areas to see shows.

Elvis performed to sold-out crowds on three different occasions. He was to perform a fourth time, but unfortunately he passed away before the scheduled event. That concert also had sold out in advance.

Dedication to detail, one of Loretta's hallmarks, was on full display while she served on the VBCC board. When they announced that tickets to a Kenny Rogers concert would go on sale, she decided she wanted to understand the general public's ticket-buying experience.

Her daughter, Sarah, wanted tickets to the concert for her birthday, but Loretta did not receive special privileges from being on the board. Securing tickets at that time required physical presence, unlike today with the ability to log online from anywhere and buy them quickly. People camped out at the box office to get a spot in line for tickets to the concert.

Loretta arrived at the VBCC with a cooler, bean bag chair, food and a portable television at 10 a.m. on a Sunday morning. She was third in line. Tickets would go on sale at 9 a.m. on Monday morning. So she, along with many others, stayed outside overnight waiting for tickets sales to begin. Tom Thrasher, chairman of the VBCC board, stopped by to check on her.

During Loretta's 20-year tenure on the VBCC board, the Huntsville Convention & Visitors Bureau was formed and housed in the VBCC for many years. The bureau merged in later years with Madison County's counterpart to become the Huntsville/Madison County Convention & Visitors Bureau.

Throughout Loretta's years in public office, she continued to focus on the Von Braun Center (VBC), as it is known today, and the Convention & Visitors Bureau. She knew the value of providing entertainment options for citizens and the potential fiscal impact of bringing conventions and events to Huntsville to draw more visitors to the city. Entertainment is a quality-of-life component, and quality of life helps drive the economy.

The VBC enabled Huntsville to host big-name entertainers, sporting events and a variety of other events for the region. Of course, its success meant it needed to expand. Also, over the years, the facility became dated and in need of improvements.

Mayor Spencer asked U.S. Sen. Richard Shelby and U.S. Rep. Bud Cramer to tour the facility to observe its condition and consider the necessary renovations and revitalizations. The lawmakers were able to secure federal dollars for some of those improvements.

Private dollars also played an important role. Propst Arena and the Mark C. Smith Concert Hall are named for the families who gave generous donations to upgrade those facilities.

Taxes from spending nights in hotels, meals at restaurants and purchases from local retail make a significant difference not only for the individual businesses but also for Huntsville as a whole. Regional and national conventions and conferences generated new money that could be used for city operations. As a volunteer and then as mayor, Loretta Spencer never lost sight of the importance of this revenue.

Chapter Four

Stepping into Politics

To be successful in politics – as a candidate or as an elected official – you must have a good team supporting you.

Loretta's background gave her an intuitive understanding of this fact. She had grown up in a tightly knit family and community where teamwork was valued and expected. Her achievements as a volunteer for various community organizations reinforced the importance of operating with a strong team.

When Ronnie Flippo made his first run for the U.S. House of Representatives in 1976, Loretta used her knowledge, experience and talent for bringing effective teams together to support his campaign. She also began to earn a reputation as a valuable political partner.

A former iron worker from Florence, Flippo had worked his way through college to earn a Bachelor of Science degree in accounting from the University of North Alabama and a master's degree from the University of Alabama. He successfully ran for a seat in the Alabama House of Representatives in 1970. After serving one term, he ran and won a seat in the Alabama Senate. However, he was not a seasoned politician for a national stage.

Loretta was serving as president of the Boys Club board of directors when Flippo asked if she would help run his campaign. He already knew that she could introduce him to people who could support his campaign, but he might not have been fully aware of her attention to details, one of her secrets to success in any endeavor.

Flippo's opponent in the run-off election was a successful lawyer from Decatur who understood the importance of dressing for the position he wanted. Loretta knew the value of being dressed appropriately for all occasions, but she also knew that Flippo had a large family of six children. Buying new suits might not be at the top of his financial priority list.

But Flippo had to make a good impression on the voters. So, Loretta contacted Bill Fowler, who owned a men's clothing business, Bill's Menswear, in Huntsville. Fowler was known to be a successful and generous businessman. He provided two nice suits, one dark, another lighter. She promised to buy shirts, ties and shoes, equipping Flippo with the clothing expected of a person seeking national office.

Loretta understood that, in the political arena, overlooking the smallest of details can be seen as a weakness. More than once, she called on a dry cleaner in Dunnavant's Mall, where she did business, to do last-minute pressings of Flippo's suits.

If Loretta was not born with her talent for persuading people to join her projects, she certainly developed the skill early in life. Convincing people to help her present the future congressman in a good light was further evidence that the community would come together to support efforts they believed in. It also gave her more experience in asking others for favors.

Political candidates and campaigns must connect with people face to face. This was even more important in those days long before social media became a huge factor. Campaigns carefully scheduled community visits so the candidates could meet as many potential voters as possible.

Loretta organized many appearances and forums for Flippo during his run-off campaigns. He often would stand on the courthouse steps in different North Alabama counties and towns talking with groups and individuals about what he wanted to accomplish as a public servant. Loretta also arranged a Campaign Kickoff Breakfast in the meeting room at Gibson's Restaurant.

Connecting Flippo with potential supporters was another important aspect of campaigning. After he won the run-off election, Loretta introduced him to key people with the Army and NASA to brief him on issues and needs impacting Redstone Arsenal. When Flippo got to Congress, he would be ready.

Campaigning for Flippo involved lots of travel, and Loretta's children, Sarah and J, joined most of these trips. The Spencer family's motorhome became a real home as they traveled to small communities. J wired some of his speakers to the top of the motorhome. It was an innovative, cost-effective and easy way to let people know that Flippo had come to town to meet and talk with people.

Sarah was in eighth grade at Randolph School during the campaign. As president of the Student Government Association, she organized a forum which all nine candidates attended during the general election before the top candidates made it to a run-off race.

Loretta enjoyed having her children with her on the campaign trail. She realized they could learn many valuable lessons from seeing democracy in action, including the importance of voting.

Flippo's political career spanned two decades, taking him from the Alabama Legislature to the U.S. Congress. He served in the U.S. House of Representatives until 1991, when he retired.

Mayor Spencer talks to U.S. Rep. Bud Cramer
at a Marshall Space Flight Center event.

When Flippo contacted Loretta to let her know that he would not be seeking re-election after his last term, she knew which person she wanted to fill his seat – Madison County District Attorney Robert E. "Bud" Cramer Jr. So, she called Cramer and told him, "Get your running shoes on." Cramer won the 5th District race that year and served in the U.S. House of Representatives until he retired in 2009.

The Flippo campaign experience with its long, tiring but ultimately successful days provided a tremendous training ground for Loretta's mayoral campaigns. She knew the work involved and the sacrifices required not only during the campaign, but also while in office. It also aligned her with a winning campaign.

Chapter Five

Economic Development

*L*oretta Spencer had long been involved in the welfare of her community in one way or another, but in March 1977, she took a more direct role in Huntsville's economic development when then-Mayor Joe Davis appointed her to the Huntsville Planning Commission. She became chair of the commission in 1981.

For some time, city leaders had been focused on attracting foreign companies that could bring manufacturing jobs to the area. About 75 percent of Huntsville's economy was dependent on the federal government – including Redstone Arsenal and NASA's Marshall Space Flight Center – with only about 25 percent coming from manufacturing. They hoped to achieve a more balanced outlook.

Starting in the 1970s, Loretta had been learning the ropes of industrial recruiting from Guy Nerren, president and general manager of the Industrial Development Board Huntsville/Madison County from 1961-1990. He stressed the need to diversify recruiting. He also taught her that the most important aspect was following through on agreements.

Loretta's varied life experiences became her economic development assets as well. Her mother had taught her the skills of warm Southern hospitality and a community service ethic. Volunteering with nonprofit organizations around town honed her natural talent for persuasion and reinforced the need to keep to a reasonable budget. Also important, as she knew from working on Ronnie Flippo's run-off campaign for Congress in 1976, were the small details that many overlook.

All of these lessons came into play when Gold Star, the South Korean electronics company which later became LG Electronics, explored building a Huntsville location in 1982.

Economic development never happens overnight. Behind each public announcement of a new company's arrival stands a sustained effort, sometimes spanning years. The courting of Gold Star involved many carefully planned events to showcase Huntsville to company executives, including the company's president, Dr. S.K. Huh.

On one of Gold Star's first visits, Loretta helped organize a dinner at The University of Alabama in Huntsville (UAH) with women from Huntsville's South Korean community who were married to UAH professors. The Korean women planned the meal, so it was authentic. They also hosted the event at the university to demonstrate the strength of the Korean community that already called Huntsville home. To further showcase the city's international flavor, they wore traditional Korean dress for the evening.

As Gold Star's interest in Huntsville continued, a group of Huntsville business leaders, including Gene and Jane Monroe, W.F. and Paula Sanders, Bob and Barbara Ward, and Guy and Loretta Spencer, entertained delegations on several occasions with Southern hospitality. Gene Monroe, W.F. Sanders, Bob Ward and Guy Spencer were members of the Economic Development Board.

Loretta always loved to entertain people in their home. When she welcomed the South Korean delegation to the Spencer home on Echols Avenue, she served coquille Saint Jacques as an appetizer before the group went to dinner in the city. Having done her cultural research, she knew that scallops and pine nuts were a favorite South Korean dish. As an added touch, she wore ginkgo earrings as an acknowledgement that the ginkgo tree is treasured in South Korea.

Despite Loretta's painstaking preparations, this cocktail and appetizer reception came with a few challenges she couldn't prevent. There was no dining table at the Spencer home for this occasion because it had been sent to be refinished. However, her knowledge of the company, her welcoming details and her "whatever it takes" attitude made a positive impression.

After the reception, the group headed to the Hilton for dinner, American music and dancing. Loretta and five members of the delegation enjoyed dancing until late into the evening. President Huh did not dance, but he did stay until the evening's end. He recognized that she was investing this time in welcoming him and his delegation. Friendliness is a gift and can put everyone on the same scale.

Everyone recognized Loretta's hospitality, but few realized she was smiling through physical pain. She had fallen while skiing earlier in March and injured her right arm. Persistent pain was a hindrance during the rigorous schedule of the Gold Star visit. She went to her doctor, and he gave her a cortisone shot which locked her arm and left it basically useless. Once again, she was thankful to be left-handed so she could prepare the appetizers.

On another occasion, the Gold Star group was entertained with a dinner in a smaller room at the VBCC. To extend an even warmer welcome, Loretta arranged for a 12-year-old Korean boy, a member of the Huntsville Youth Orchestra, to play the violin. Since it was a more intimate dinner, she felt like music would be a nice touch. The beauty of his performance moved President Huh to tears – the perfect end to the evening.

The young violinist's moving performance was perhaps his last in Huntsville. The boy's father was a professor at UAH, and the family was leaving two weeks later to move to Houston. Timing can be everything.

During that same visit, the delegation was treated to a brunch the next day while Huntsville's art culture was being showcased at the annual Panoply of the Arts festival. By coincidence, the delegation walked out of the VBCC door and saw a group of young people with their instructor performing Tae Kwon Do. The group dedicated their exhibition to Dr. Huh.

The agreement with Gold Star was finalized that weekend. They chose a site, and Gold Star executives were excited to have the property near the airport. The International Intermodal Center would make it possible for Gold Star to ship directly to that point without having to go through customs in Atlanta – a 15-hour flight from South Korea.

The Gold Star delegation's itinerary was a whirlwind experience, showcasing Huntsville's quality health care, arts, schools and retail offerings. But Loretta always made time to make personal connections and establish relationships.

It was very important to have a translator to make sure there was accurate communication between all parties to build trust for future relationships. Dr. Huh had an excellent translator who was fondly remembered in Huntsville as a gentleman who favored wearing a trench coat in the style of the popular television detective Columbo. The South Korean delegation made personal connections that would span many years.

Gold Star quickly became a valued corporate citizen in Huntsville. Loretta recalls that they loved selling their televisions at good prices for gifts, and they offered factory-direct sales to the public.

On one occasion, Loretta purchased a television as a wedding gift for the daughter of Ray Bass, the director of the state highway department. She had asked him to be the keynote speaker for the Chamber of Commerce's annual trip to Montgomery to meet with legislators. Then-Gov. George Wallace had made the position of highway department director a permanent one instead of an appointed position.

Bass appreciated Loretta's thoughtfulness for his daughter, and the gesture helped strengthen their rapport. When she was presenting the gift, it just happened to come up in the conversation about the status of Huntsville's roadway capital plan submission. Bass told Loretta and Ernest Kaufman, then the City Council president, that the paperwork had not been submitted yet and was due in two weeks in order for the city to be considered for federal funding for future highways. That heads-up proved beneficial in making sure that the appropriate documents were submitted on time. The governor met with them and signed the papers that day.

Gold Star was so impressed with Huntsville, according to a New York Times article on Oct. 5, 1982, that, in addition to the factory, they were also "developing plans for three other factories in a 50-acre area of Huntsville."

Huntsville leaders continued to impress Gold Star with hospitality to strengthen relations with company leadership in the days leading up to the plant's ribbon-cutting in 1983. One of the more public events was a gala dinner held at the VBCC the evening before the ribbon-cutting. Guy

Nerren asked Loretta to chair the organization of the dinner, which had a guest list of more than 200 people.

When Loretta asked about the budget for the event, Nerren inquired of President Huh, who replied "unlimited." Loretta reminded Nerren that volunteers did not work without a budget. "Unlimited" was still the response.

Bottled for Gold Star of America

To celebrate Gold Star's decision to open a manufacturing facility in Huntsville, Loretta Spencer had custom labels created using the Gold Star logo. The labels were affixed to jeroboams of champagne at the gala dinner.

Loretta felt the weight of their trust, which spurred her to make the event the best it could be – on her own budget.

To give the blank canvas of the East Hall a more elegant ambience, Loretta arranged for an outdoor billboard emblazoned with Gold Star's logo to be rolled into the hall. Parisian, a well-known retail store at the time, provided gold Mylar table toppers. The son of Dr. John Wright, then-president of UAH, printed special labels with Gold Star's logo for the jeroboams of champagne.

Loretta's volunteer background shines through in these preparations, which were donated to the cause of economic development. She was never too shy to ask the community to get involved with big events as opportunities to donate. This was one of many times that Huntsville came together to support similar efforts.

That evening, long-stem roses were presented to the ladies. When it came time to toast the official arrival of Gold Star to Huntsville, Mayor Davis, County Commission Chairman James Record, President Huh and two other South Korean dignitaries popped the champagne corks in unison.

There were so many details garnered from different businesses to make this event successful and memorable. Interestingly, this formal banquet cost less than the price of the box lunches for the ribbon-cutting held the next day at the plant's opening celebration.

One of Loretta's most cherished memories of that evening was talking with Mrs. Huh and meeting her lady-in-waiting. Mrs. Huh wished to give Loretta a traditional Korean dress. Her lady-in-waiting just looked at Loretta and was able to discern size and dimensions. When the dress arrived, it was a perfect fit. This gift was so special that Loretta has kept it to this day.

Gold Star President Huh was so pleased with everything done to welcome them to Huntsville that he invited Loretta to visit South Korea. He said that, if she would fly to Japan, he would send his personal plane for the trip from Japan to South Korea to visit Gold Star there. Loretta appreciated the invitation, but she was concerned about the extensive flight time. When a follow-up invitation came, she encouraged Guy Spencer to go with Guy Nerren in her place.

Successfully putting together an international business deal of this magnitude requires extensive precision and attention to detail. It's not easy, even with the advanced communications technology of today. In the 1980s, this was all done without the ease of cellphones, email and texts. All questions had to be cabled to South Korea.

In November 1985, Gold Star reached the milestone of 1 million televisions. By the late 1980s, the company was reported to be producing more than a million televisions and microwaves annually.

LG Electronics began as Gold Star, which Loretta Spencer helped bring to Huntsville during her days as a civic volunteer.

The relationship Loretta helped to forge with Gold Star continues to benefit the North Alabama region with announcements by LG Electronics in 2018 of expanded operations and added jobs.

HUNTSVILLE
the Sky is not the limit.®

Key Factors in Economic Development

1944	Formation of Huntsville Industrial Expansion Committee (HIEC)
1949	U. S. Army designates Redstone Arsenal as center for rocket and guided missile projects
1950	German rocket team led by Dr. Wernher von Braun comes to Huntsville from Fort Bliss, Texas
1952	Activation of U.S. Army Ordnance Guided Missle School, now the U.S. Army Ordnance Missile and Munitions Center & School
1955	An Alabama business corporation known as Huntsville Industrial Sites (HIS), Inc. is organized to make land available to industrial concerns. HIS purchased 248 acres of land the next year
1956	Activation of Army Ballistic Missile Agency (ABMA)
1958	Activation of Army Ordnance Missile Command, now U.S. Army Missile Command (MICOM)
1960	Activation of NASA Marshall Space Flight Center with transfer of some 4,000 civilian specialists from ABMA and Wernher von Braun as director of NASA/MSFC
1962	The University of Alabama Research Institute in Huntsville is formed with a $3 million bond issue
1964	The University of Alabama announced the establishment of a four-year curriculum at the Huntsville campus. HIS, Inc. name is changed to The University of Alabama/Huntsville Foundation
1965	General Electric is the first company, in Huntsville, to use industrial revenue bond financing as provided for in the Cater Act
1965	Beginning of industrial diversification efforts with emphasis on companies not depending on missle and space contracts
1967	Activation of U.S. Army Corps of Engineers Huntsville Division
1970	Opening of the U.S. Space & Rocket Center
1975	HIEC is renamed Industrial Development Association (IDA)

Chamber of Commerce • Huntsville/Madison County
225 CHURCH STREET, NW • POST OFFICE BOX 408 • HUNTSVILLE, ALABAMA 35804-0408 • 205-535-2000

"Key Factors in Economic Development" from the Chamber of Commerce of Huntsville/Madison County, page 1.

1975	Activation of the U.S. Army Strategic Defense Command as a major element of the U.S. Strategic Defense Initiative
1980	Consolidation of IDA and Chamber of Commerce into the Chamber of Commerce Huntsville/Madison County as the community's primary economic development agency
1980	Beginning of an unprecedented general economic boom with wide range of investments
1980	Approval of U.S. Customs Port of Entry (Code 1910) at Huntsville International Airport
1982	Opening of U.S. Space Camp/U.S. Space Academy as part of the U.S. Space & Rocket Center
1983	Approval of Foreign Trade Zone No. 83 under the management of the Huntsville/Madison County Airport Authority
1983	Formation of the Madison County Office of Planning and Economic Development
1986	Opening of the International Intermodal Center in the Foreign Trade Zone. This facility provides transfer of intermodal containers between air, rail and truck
1987	NorthEast Alabama Regional Small Business Development Center moves into the Chamber of Commerce building and becomes an partner in economic development
1988	Alabama Supercomputer Network becomes active with its headquarters in Huntsville's Cummings Research Park
1989	Wages of Huntsville and Madison County residents averaged $24,445, according to the U.S. Department of Labor, putting the area at the top of 63 metropolitan areas in the seven-state region
1990	Huntsville was Alabama's fastest growing urban area during the 1980's, a decade that saw three of the state's 11 metropolitan centers lose population, according to the Census Bureau
1990	The Army Missile Command now manages numerous weapons systems such as the Patriot, Hellfire, MLRS (Multiple Launch Rocket System) Army Tactical Missile System, TOW and all other tactical missiles and rockets, and manages 200 major contractors and hundreds of subcontractors, was named the Army's most productive and best managed research facility for 1990
1991	The more than $50 million renovation of Huntsville International Airport was completed in 1991. Major additions included the new two-level concourse with jetways. The initial concourse can accomodate ten large jet airloading bridges and four commuter aircraft positions
	The Interstate (I-565) was completed and connects the eastern part of the county with Interstate 65

"Key Factors in Economic Development" from the Chamber of Commerce of Huntsville/Madison County, page 2.

Chapter Six

Cummings Research Park

*Loretta Spencer played a significant role in the development
and growth of Cummings Research Park (CRP)
as a member of the Huntsville Planning Commission.*

$\mathcal{C}$ummings Research Park (CRP) looms large over Huntsville's economic landscape. As of 2024, it is the second largest research park in the U.S. and the fourth largest in the world. Combining Fortune 500 companies, local and international high-tech enterprises, U.S. space and defense agencies, thriving business incubators and competitive higher-education institutions, it is one of the world's leading science and technology business parks. More than 300 companies, 26,000-plus employees and some 13,500 students call it home.

As a member of the Huntsville Planning Commission, Loretta played a significant role in establishing the standards that contributed to the park's success.

She recalls that the area the park now occupies was strikingly different in the early 1960s. Then the land was a canvas of hundreds of acres of rolling farmland marked only by an unpaved road, eventually named Sparkman Drive.

The establishment in 1962 of Huntsville Research Park, as Cummings Research Park was first called, grew out of a conversation between a group of Huntsville community leaders and Dr. Wernher von Braun, leader of the rocket team on Redstone Arsenal. They were seeking ways the city could create a collaborative environment for companies that supported the groundbreaking research happening on the arsenal.

The park's first occupant was Brown Engineering. Milton K. Cummings, the company's founder, and Joe Moquin, its vice president, bought a 100-acre lot in 1962 at the end of that unpaved road for the company's new corporate office. Brown Engineering became Teledyne Brown Engineering in 1967 when Teledyne Inc. of Los Angeles bought the engineering firm.

In its early days, the park lacked cohesive development standards, Loretta recalls. There were some major companies in the park at this time, but they were not necessarily in a hurry to build to occupy the land they held. As the companies won contracts, they would add buildings.

Milton Cummings died in 1973, and Huntsville Research Park was renamed Cummings Research Park in his honor. The original park, CRP East, filled up by the late 1980s. The City of Huntsville purchased additional land in 1982, and today this is known as CRP West.

As with most projects of this size and detail, CRP West began with a bit of controversy and political push and pull. Loretta helped smooth out those wrinkles and keep the project on track.

David Moore, the owner of the land where the park was growing, wanted the land to be used for more residential construction with apart-

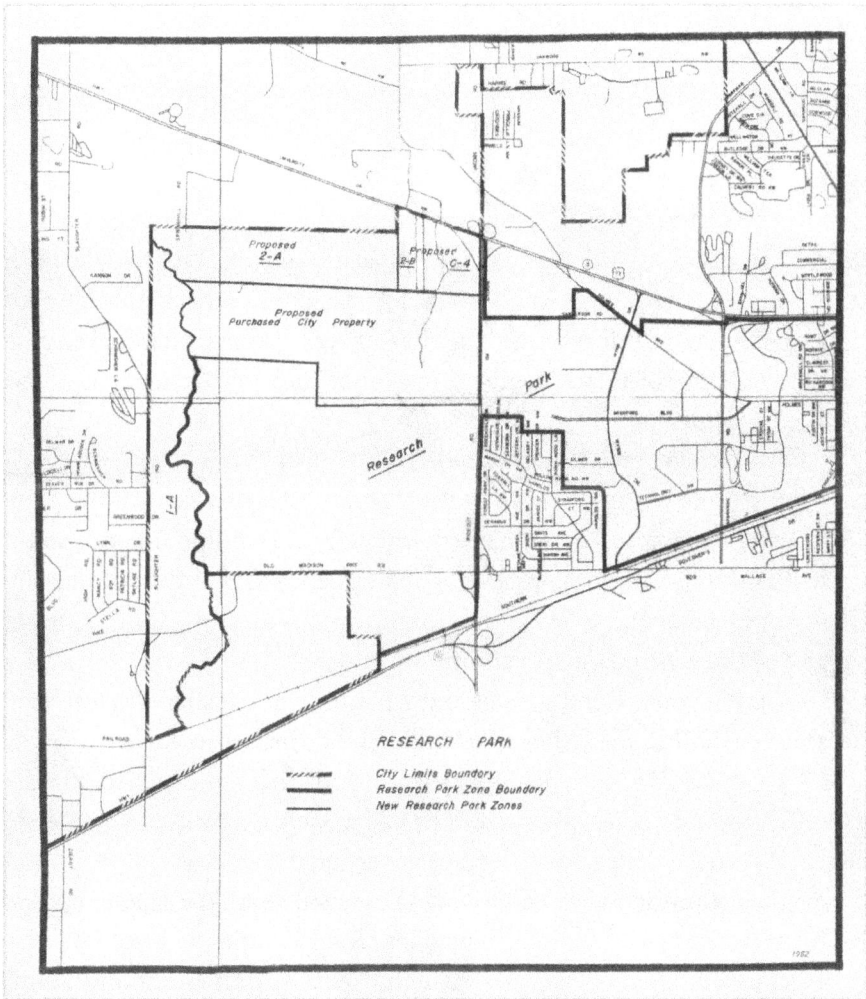

*This map shows the area the City of Huntsville wished to acquire
for the expansion of Cummings Research Park West.*

ments and shopping. He said that he could not sell it for his preferred
development under the research park zoning. He urged Mayor Davis to
change the zoning to allow apartments.

Loretta was chair of the Huntsville Planning Commission by this
time, and she knew she had to convince Davis to develop the land in support of the Cummings Research Park vision. Her long acquaintance with

Davis – she had been a student when Davis was principal of her middle school – would certainly help, as would her many civic volunteer experiences. Volunteers, she knew, sometimes have a great advantage in swaying political movements, and many decisions are made on the golf course as well as over a meal or two.

It took conversations over two meals of catfish at the old Greenbrier Restaurant in addition to picking turnip greens at Davis's farm in New Market to win him over. Loretta's persistence convinced him to let them gather more information. She has never underestimated the value of strong personal relationships, but sometimes persuasion has to be handled carefully.

One of the people Loretta needed on her fact-finding team was Dallas Fanning. He began working in the Planning Department in the early 1970s after serving in Vietnam. Two years after Davis appointed Loretta to the Planning Commission, several board members pointed out that the Planning Department director did not have a degree in planning. Loretta suggested the well-qualified Fanning for the job.

(Another time Loretta recognized Fanning as a leader was after she became mayor. He made her aware that the governor had the option to award a General's Star to qualified members of the National Guard. She called Gov. Fob James and found out he had already committed to someone else. So, when Don Siegelman became governor, she made another call, and during the conversation he said he would be glad to award the star to Fanning for his service as well as his continued leadership in the National Guard.)

Loretta wanted to travel to Raleigh, North Carolina, and meet with Research Triangle staff to gather more detailed information on developing a research park of this size. However, Fanning told her that he could not be the one to ask Mayor Davis about making the trip. He worked for Davis and could not take the risk of opposing his boss.

Loretta told Mayor Davis she would pay her own way to Raleigh if he would let some employees go with her. Fanning; Ralph Gipson, assistant to the mayor; Bob Ward, managing editor of The Huntsville Times, and a female Times reporter accompanied her. This fact-finding mission continues to pay off tremendously for Huntsville and the surrounding region.

The Research Triangle director and staff shared information about the structure of The Triangle and amenities to make it a premier park. They advised the Huntsville group to considering all aesthetic features by developing landscaping standards, requiring underground utilities and forbidding the installation of HVAC systems on top of buildings. This would result in a well-maintained area resembling a college campus. The parking areas were to have berms so parked vehicles would not obscure the meticulous landscaping.

Research Triangle representatives suggested that they include wide sidewalks to allow anyone who worked in the park to walk or jog there during lunch or off time. They also recommended that the size of site locations be two-to-five acres. Zoning requirements that would not allow any manufacturing was another stipulation.

The board would set the standards and maintain them. It would be the city's reputation that would be held accountable to maintain the research park name and designation.

Loretta's group came back with a great deal of detailed information and advice. They faced a huge task to transform the land in a way that would attract top employers.

Loretta was responsible for forming the initial Cummings Research Park Board. She chose Guy Nerren because he was the director of the Industrial Development Board as well as Olin King, Gene Monroe, Joe Moquin, W.F. Sanders Jr., Bob Ward, and Carol Ann Samples and Jean Watts, daughters of Milton Cummings. A City Council member also alternated on the board. Other members included the mayor's administrative assistant Gipson plus the city attorney and Planning Department staff.

The CRP Board understood the importance of good aesthetics and established a design review board to insure that architecture would meet required standards.

On one occasion Ernest Kaufman, president of the City Council at the time, alerted Loretta to a potential problem with a construction project in Research Park. Instead of the required underground wiring, the contractor was installing overhead wiring. Loretta immediately talked with Mayor Davis. She reminded him that underground wiring had been

THE EDITORIAL PAGE OF

The Huntsville Times

For Truth, Progress and Independence

Established March 23, 1910

P.O. Box 1487, Huntsville, Ala. 35807 (205) 532-4000 USPS 254—640

Leroy A. Simms, *Editor and Publisher*

Patrick McCauley, *Executive Editor*   Clyde Lewis, *Comptroller*
Bob Ward, *Managing Editor*   Hubert C. Hawkins, *Marketing Mgr.*
Raymond Johnson, *Production Mgr.*   Virginia Bowers, *Advertising Mgr.*
Carlos Kirkpatrick, *Circulation Mgr.*   Buford Bagwell, *Classified Ad Mgr.*

HUNTSVILLE, AL   WEDNESDAY, MARCH 10, 1982

Making the Most of It

How to maximize the benefits — that perennial question is at the heart of the deliberations for city purchase of 617 acres of land in Cummings Research Park and rezoning of some 375 acres of park-zoned property for residential and commercial development.

The interest and the talks are intense, for the stakes are high. Several million dollars would be involved in the purchase and the development. More importantly, Huntsville's economic well-being will be greatly influenced by the outcome.

In question are almost 1,000 acres of land owned by Floyd Moore and Moore family members. For two decades the land has been zoned for research industry, and that was all right with Moore as long as he farmed most of it. But he has retired from farming now and wants to enjoy the benefits of the land in a different way, by sale and development. He has other offers, in fact, for non-research development of sizable portions of this property next to the existing park.

Moore's interests, of course, are not the only thing at stake here. Research Park has proved an immense asset to the community over the years. Some of our most valued industries are situated on the approximately 600 acres developed or already held there so far, and less than 150 acres — in mostly small, odd-shaped tracts — are actually available in the existing park for sale to new and expanding industries.

Moreover, the wave of future industrial development in high technology makes the remaining 2,600 undeveloped acres Huntsville's ace in the hole. Thus, the integrity of Research Park is very much a community interest.

A crucial long-range decision that must be made by the City Council is whether to continue to reserve the whole park-zoned tract — between University and Governors drives and westward from Rideout Road to Indian creek — for research industries, or whether some of the acreage can and should be developed for residential and commercial uses to meet a balanced range of needs.

At the moment, however, discussion centers on a proposal by Moore to sell the city 617 acres for something more than $3 million and to retain 375 acres along University Drive for residential and commercial development. The proposal includes conditions and specifications that would preserve the integrity of Research Park and provide access to the industrial, commercial and residential areas.

While big money is involved, it seems a fair price, judging from recent land sales in the vicinity and the going rate generally for industrial property. The transaction can be financed by tax-free municipal bonds and should in the end return some profit to the city as Research Park is developed further and the land is sold. The city's tax revenues also stand to gain from future industrial development and additional jobs.

Several alternatives have been considered. Too, the question of precedent must be weighed, for some 1,500 acres south of the Moore tract remain in private ownership and could in the future require a solution.

But that acreage is not at issue now. The decision that is at hand bears directly and immediately upon Huntsville's participation in the high-tech future. The City Council has had two weeks to consider this specific Moore proposal, and the question of rezoning that acreage has been before municipal authorities for almost a full year.

The matter cries out for resolution, and promptly. It cries out for vision on the part of the city's elected leaders. Shortsightedness or negativism at this point would serve only to damage this community's progressive, forward-looking reputation and severely restrict its future opportunities. Given the need to accommodate a variety of legitimate private and community interests, the Moore offer to sell part and retain part of this land seems sound and fair.

In this clipping from Mayor Spencer's scrapbooks, The Huntsville Times' editorial board urges a compromise between landowner and city in the effort to expand Cummings Research Park West.

stressed as an important aesthetic element for attracting companies to locate there.

As for landowner Moore, Davis worked with him to include diversity of land use with some apartments permitted, and the initial community, Rime Village, was developed.

The city maintained ownership of CRP property so they could sell the land. This presented the opportunity to purchase additional tracts of land when they became available. Thus, a good inventory was kept for companies wanting to locate in the park in the future.

A percentage of the sale of the land was set aside to purchase other parcels. When additional companies wanted to build in CRP, the regulations would continue to be required.

The initial fact-finding group that met with those instrumental in the Research Triangle formation understood the importance of setting a standard and sticking with it. Even though the Chamber of Commerce now markets the land, the City Council controls the use.

Dynetics was the first company to open in CRP West. CAS was the second company to occupy brick and mortar in the western park.

Cummings Research Park is now an economic driver in the Tennessee Valley region. When Loretta became Mayor Spencer, she remarked about its success, "With each company, our reputation grew."

More than 27,000 individuals travel from areas in the Tennessee Valley region to work for the 300 companies occupying the park. The location of The University of Alabama in Huntsville (UAH) and Calhoun Community College also attracts more than 13,000 students to the park. The impact of the park has an exponential effect on the quality of life for those employed there as well as the region as a whole.

An important factor in CRP's growth and success is the Bradford Drive bridge that overpasses Research Park Boulevard. Loretta understood the need to easily connect the two sections of the park, and she addressed the matter with the CRP Board and went to Montgomery and spoke directly to Mack Roberts, director of the Alabama Department of Transportation.

"It would never have become the second largest research park in the U.S. without that bridge," she said, "because it tied the east and west sides of the park."

Loretta asked Mark Smith, founder and CEO of ADTRAN, if she could host a reception to thank Roberts and ALDOT for making the bridge possible. Smith graciously made one of his conference rooms available, and the event included the CEOs of other CRP companies who also recognized the impact of the bridge.

As a special thank you, Loretta presented Roberts with a pen set carved out of Chittamwood by a surgeon at Huntsville Hospital and an Auburn basketball signed by the team.

"I knew Mack Roberts had a weakness for Auburn basketball," she said.

As a volunteer and as the mayor, Loretta always remembered that thoughtful, personal gifts can never be underestimated.

STATE OF ALABAMA

GOVERNOR'S OFFICE

MONTGOMERY 36130

GEORGE C. WALLACE
GOVERNOR

October 5, 1984

Ms. Loretta Spencer, Chairman
City of Huntsville Planning Commission
P.O. Box 308
Huntsville, Alabama   35804

Dear Ms. Spencer:

Thank you for your letter of August 28, 1984, concerning the proposed project for Bradford Drive access to Rideout Road.

The Highway Department has made studies concerning this project, therefore, I am referring this letter to Highway Director, Ray D. Bass, for reply.

I assure you that I am vitally interested in the development in the Huntsville area, and will continue to give the officials in your area any support that is necessary to insure that this growth continues.

With kind personal regards, I am

Sincerely yours,

George C. Wallace

GCW:adj

*Governor George C. Wallace expressed his support for the
Bradford Drive overpass in this letter.*

For Cummings Research Park to receive its proper recognition, Loretta understood that it was very important for the road leading to it to be renamed Research Park Boulevard. It was a practical matter as well; renaming the road would let drivers on Interstate 565 know which exits to take to reach CRP.

People who didn't live in this area at the time might think that the road and the park were named simultaneously. However, longer residents will remember the previous name, Rideout Road. The Alabama Department of Transportation was not too keen on renaming it at first. However, after discussions with Mayor Spencer, they too saw the value for people doing business in the park.

Sign of change: Rideout Road is now Research Park Boulevard

Mayor Spencer, second from left in line, stands with area officials to mark the renaming of Rideout Road to Research Park Boulevard.

In 1997, after being elected mayor, Loretta and the City Council made changes in how the land was sold to provide maintenance for CRP. This was something that had not been provided for earlier. One change required that 15 percent of the selling price of each parcel of land would go into a fund to provide landscaping and maintenance to keep CRP at a high standard of excellence.

Chamber Chairman Gary Pledger, CRP Director Bill Dean, Huntsville Mayor Loretta Spencer, and UAH Vice President of Research Dr. Ken Harwell announce the award given to CRP during a recent press conference.

Cummings Research Park Presented International Award For Excellence

Huntsville's Cummings Research Park (CRP) was recently recognized by the Association of University Related Research Parks (AURRP) during the organization's annual awards for excellence in Research Park Development and Practice. CRP was awarded The Outstanding Research Park Achievement Award at the 12th Annual AURRP International Conference to recognize the best the world has to offer in Monterey, Calif.

Founded in 1986, AURRP is recognized as the preeminent international organization serving university related parks and technology incubators around the world. Research and technology parks help bring technology from the laboratory to economically viable business activities and thus make an important contribution to business volume, jobs, and public revenue growth in their communities. Their active participation in the university community also has an important positive effect on university research funding success and on student and faculty recruitment.

"While CRP is recognized as one of the oldest and largest U.S. research parks, The Outstanding Research Park Achievement Award acknowledges Huntsville's technology infrastructure that has over time successfully developed a high performing and sustainable regional economy," CRP Director Bill Dean said.

"I have watched the progress and growth of this park for the past 30 years and this award is something our community can be very proud of," Huntsville Mayor Loretta Spencer commented. "Cummings Research Park has been recognized as the most outstanding in the world by an eminent association. The success of the park is the result of foresight by our city fathers and the courage of the entrepreneurs who chose to locate there."

CRP was established in 1962 and occupies over 7 million square feet of building space on 3800 acres of research and development zoned property. The University of Alabama in Huntsville and Calhoun Community College are located in the park as well as 180 companies employing over 220,000 people. The park provides an excellent environment for business and technology, which fosters advanced educational standards and a high quality of life.

Aug 3, 1997

Chapter Seven

First Bid for Mayor

The 1996 Huntsville mayoral race drew a crowded field. Steve Hettinger, who had served as mayor from 1988 to 1996, announced that he would not seek a third term. Twelve people announced their campaign intentions, including Loretta Purdy Spencer. One of her 11 rivals dropped out, but another person signed up, keeping 12 candidates in the race.

"I know all of this community," Loretta told reporter Keith Clines of The Huntsville Times when she entered the race. "The different efforts I've worked on have carried me to every quadrant. I want to bring that background to the mayor's office. I love people and I love making things happen. I couldn't care less who gets credit for it."

Loretta faced strong competition: Ken Arnold, Randy Bounds, Glenn Bracken, Walter Coots, Will Culver, Herb Dixon, John Dodd, Larry Mullins, Dean O'Farrell, Joe Perkins, Jackie Reed and Rob White. Each of those individuals brought different experiences and qualifications to the race.

The mayoral race largely focused on the topics of unity, religion, public safety and economics, according to an article about a well-attended community forum published in the Tuesday, July 9, 1996, issue of The Huntsville Times. As the campaign progressed, other issues rose to the surface, such as the candidates' opinions on commitments made by the previous administration, including Huntsville's role in paying for a new public safety complex, building a new art museum, improving roads, pursuing automated garbage pickups and improving relations between the mayor and the City Council.

Loretta's campaign style reflected her approach to conducting business as mayor. Her written schedule was full of meet-and-greets with civic groups, organizations and neighborhood associations as well as participation in forums and town hall meetings. In her spare time, she pursued a relentless quest to knock on every door in Huntsville to meet residents and hear what was important to them. Years later, she would recall the many pairs of shoes that she wore out on that campaign trail.

"Listening to people is what it's all about," she told Clines for an article that appeared in The Times' Aug. 12, 1996, edition. "She starts early and ends late," Clines wrote, "squeezing in as many stops as possible."

She was trying to make the most efficient use of her time, another characteristic that she would carry into City Hall.

Loretta's campaign message offered Huntsville voters straightforward priorities:

- Bring vision and unity to Huntsville.
- Enhance and diversify the tax base to provide more city services.
- Bring in retail and new businesses (high tech, excluding paper mills and other companies posing environmental problems).
- Improve city beautification and maintenance.
- Work for quality education for students in all areas of Huntsville.

As the August election day drew closer, three of the eleven candidates were close in the polls. Results of the Southern Opinion Research of Tuscaloosa/Huntsville Times showed Larry Mullins leading with 26 percent, Dean O'Farrell in second with 20 percent and Loretta in third with 16 percent.

Loretta received coveted endorsements from The Huntsville Times and H-Vote, the political arm of the Huntsville Education Association and Retired Teachers of Madison County.

The Times' endorsement on Aug. 18, 1996, stated, "Huntsville is a maturing city. Its prosperity requires constant vigilance. For the community to pull together to assure its continued success, individuals and groups must put aside their differences for the benefit of all. We believe Loretta Spencer can get people to do that."

Huntsville voted for its next mayor on Aug. 27, 1996. When the votes were counted, the result required a run-off race: Loretta received the most votes with 11,141 or 32.4 percent with Larry Mullins in second at 8,844 votes or 25.7 percent. Dean O'Farrell finished third with 8,470 votes or 24.7 percent.

Loretta's hard work and the voters' response to her vision for the city put her at the top of the list. Huntsville, that city of historic firsts, was poised to elect its first female mayor and give Alabama the first female mayor of a major city.

Chapter Eight

The Run-off Race

"Fast and focused" was Loretta's description of the weeks leading up to the run-off election on Sept. 17, 1996.

Loretta and Larry Mullins began strengthening their cases the day after the general election at The Huntsville Press Club's luncheon. Loretta received endorsements from her former mayoral rivals Glenn Bracken, Walter Coots, Herb Dixon and Dean O'Farrell. Other endorsements came from the Police Benevolent Association and City Councilman Richard Showers, who was re-elected to his third term in 1996.

The initial campaign for mayor had been viewed as mostly positive; however, higher stakes brought a different tone to the run-off. Mullins and Loretta had promised each other that they would continue that earlier attitude during the run-off. While Loretta brought more groups to the table to discuss issues and earned endorsements from a diverse group, including outgoing Mayor Steve Hettinger and his wife, Bonnie, Mullins was reported to have taken a more negative tone.

The Huntsville Times reported Mullins describing Hettinger's placement of a yard sign for Loretta and statements that some department directors might continue on as "an integral part of the status quo that is carrying this city deeper and deeper into debt."

As Loretta highlighted her experience with the Planning Commission, Huntsville-Madison County Senior Center and various other organizations, Mullins tried to spin her volunteer service against her.

Loretta's experience prior to taking office was unprecedented for a Huntsville mayor. She had integral roles on the Huntsville Planning Commission and served on so many other volunteer boards: Von Braun

Civic Center, Crime Stoppers, Huntsville Housing Development, United Way, State Film Commission, Boys & Girls Club, Harris Home for Children, Huntsville Botanical Garden, Huntsville Economic Development Board, Huntsville/Madison County Convention & Visitors Board, Huntsville/Madison County Chamber of Commerce State Government Commission and Senior Center Board, just to name a few. She also was active at church and regularly taught Sunday school at First United Methodist. This combined experience provided multi-faceted insights into the community.

Mullins' attempts to turn Loretta's positive community service into a negative were unsuccessful. Loretta expanded her previous level of support, winning 45 of the city's voting precincts for a total of 22,580 votes. Mullins received 11,982 votes, winning 7 precincts. The final percentage was 65.3 percent for Loretta and 34.7 percent for Mullins.

It's Ms. Mayor now

September 18, 1996

Big winner Spencer says she's ready to start work

By KEITH CLINES
Times Staff Writer

Cake and soft drinks, chips and vegetables with dip were spread across several tables at the Huntsville-Madison County Senior Center where mayor-elect Loretta Spencer was celebrating Tuesday night.

Over to the side, lying on a table unattended while Spencer appeared on all of the local television stations' 10 o'clock news shows, was a spiral-bound book, a half-inch thick.

■ Area election results. Page B1.
■ For Mayor-elect Loretta Spencer and District 5 Councilman-elect Glenn Watson, the easy part is over. Editorial. Page B6.

The book was outgoing Mayor Steve Hettinger's proposed 1997 operating budget. A mayoral aide had given it to Spencer earlier in the evening after her landslide win over Larry Mullins.

Bryan Bacon/Huntsville Times
Loretta Spencer hugs supporter Don Sweeney during her victory celebration. The city's newly elected mayor says she will be attending budget hearings before taking a vacation.

Loretta Spencer won the run-off election on Sept. 17, 1996, with 65.3% of the vote.

After the run-off election, Mullins explained the intention behind what many people considered his negative campaign. He stated he was simply "attacking the system" and not Loretta personally, according to The Huntsville Times, Sept. 18, 1996.

It was a new day in politics for Huntsville. As Loretta prepared to take office in a few weeks on Oct. 8, 1996, she was aware of some of the challenges that lay ahead. She had existing issues to address and solutions to provide. However, there were also problems that were not public knowledge and that she didn't know about – yet.

Chapter Nine

Putting Promises into Action

ayor-elect Spencer, true to form, hit the ground running. Her fast pace from the campaign trail did not slow as she prepared to take office. On Sept. 19, 1996, she talked with several department directors and reviewed city budget requests with outgoing Mayor Hettinger's assistant and with Councilman Bill Kling. An incoming mayor inherits many things, good and bad. Since the mayor takes office during October, an incoming mayor is given the budget prepared by the former mayor and approved by the City Council.

Loretta Spencer was sworn in to office for her first term on Oct. 9, 1996, as the first female mayor of Huntsville as well as the first female mayor of one of the four largest cities in Alabama. During her inauguration speech, she called for a new beginning based on unity. To emphasize that point, her swearing-in ceremony was the first to be held outdoors to make it open to all people.

On her first day in office, she set out to fulfill her campaign promise to clean up Memorial Parkway. Local news outlets reported on the work crew that she led: volunteers from garden clubs and other organizations, all city department directors, and 75 work-release inmates. They started on the northern portion of the Parkway at the Mount Charron neighborhood and worked all the way to the southern end at Redstone Road, not too far from the Tennessee River.

When people questioned her about her first official act as mayor, she reminded them that she intended to bring new industries to Huntsville and the city had to be ready to greet them. Her experience in economic development proved beneficial to the city. As she had learned from Guy

Nerren, companies that were considering a Huntsville location would make unannounced visits to see how the city was being maintained. She was determined that the city would always be ready.

Investing in Huntsville was a consistent focus during Mayor Spencer's administrations, and maintaining a beautiful, clean city was definitely a priority. She appointed Stephanie Malone as the coordinator for Operation Green Team. Malone's track record was the perfect fit. She had worked for U.S. Rep. Bud Cramer and was well-known for her work ethic and ability to build a good network of people. As the program grew, everyone from students to business leaders learned about the importance of having a clean city for residents as well as for economic development.

To further emphasize the point that new people and businesses were welcome in Huntsville during her administration, Loretta installed the first "Welcome to Huntsville" banner flags on all major entry ways into the city. Paying attention to details as usual, she made sure that the city purchased quality flags that could be used for an extended time to get a good value for the price. The fabric had a 10-year guarantee.

As an extension of the welcome banner plan, she put lighted decorations in the shape of snowflakes in the downtown area as well as on north and south portions of Memorial Parkway. The decorations are still in use more than 25 years later from Thanksgiving until into the new year.

Loretta understood that some people might not miss the difference small details make when combined together – at least, not until they travel to a town without this focus. A welcoming atmosphere makes people want to stay longer in a city, enjoy its hospitality, spend their tourist dollars and return again. It also attracts businesses that boost the city's economic development with good jobs and tax revenue. An attractive appearance is a vital component in any city's successful growth plan.

Chapter Ten

Facing Civic and Business Challenges

ayor Spencer's first inauguration day was filled with the satisfaction of promises kept, but it also included the revelation of previously hidden problems. Few people who witnessed her take the oath of office on that Monday were aware of the news she had recently received. She had been informed on the previous Friday that a city department was under federal investigation, and she should not be surprised to learn of a raid on the city's Sewer Department during her swearing-in proceedings.

The problems with the Sewer Department didn't stop with the investigation. Later in 1997 the department's superintendent was fired, and several other employees were under scrutiny for possibly using city equipment to do private work.

However, out of this very bad situation came a positive outcome for the mayor, the city and the Sewer Department. Mayor Spencer was able to hire Tommy Lovelady, who had recently retired from the military. Not only did he have a distinguished military career, but he also had made the highest grade ever on a state exam. His tenure with what is now the Water Pollution Control Department was exemplary; he definitely left the department better than he found it. Lovelady had implemented proactive maintenance which drastically improved operations and efficiency. That maintenance also prevented the city from facing fines that other cities in the region were experiencing for negligence.

On a more basic level, Mayor Spencer quickly brought changes to City Hall's structure. City "super chiefs" would be eliminated. Instead 26 department heads would report directly to her and would become appointed instead of merit employees. She also added a communications director to effectively communicate with the public.

Spencer sells her plan

Oct 30

■ The mayor got what she wanted. And to her credit, she is willing to shoulder whatever credit or blame that results.

Huntsville Mayor Loretta Spencer won the job with about 65 percent of the vote in the September runoff. If that's not a mandate, we don't know what is. Not surprisingly, then, she got most of what she wanted in her reorganization plan for City Hall. And what she didn't get won't matter much.

Spencer's plan eliminated two of the three so-called "superchiefs" created by the council under former Mayor Steve Hettinger. The new organizational structure has the disadvantage of a lot of people answering directly to the mayor, perhaps leaving her precious little time to be out in the community. It has the advantage of giving the mayor control over the things she's responsible for. There's no longer a built-in mechanism for passing the buck.

The council, however, refused to go along with Spencer's request to put Animal Control under the police department. It is now under public services; the plan approved by the council makes the animal control director a department head, answering directly to the mayor.

Monday's meeting between the council and the mayor was a little testy at times. Spencer showed she isn't going to be cowed as the only elected woman official in city government. The council showed it takes its role seriously and won't rubber-stamp things.

The value of the mayor's organizational plan remains to be seen. If it works, it's a good plan. If it doesn't, it ought to be changed. The critical pieces of the puzzle are the people charged with carrying out these duties. Next up for Mayor Spencer: naming her department heads.

Smart, sensible, hard-working people can perform well in a variety of organizational structures. A bad structure, however, can allow the failures of one or two individuals to ruin the whole operation.

Mayor Spencer got what she wanted. It's up to her to make it work, and, to her credit, she is willing to shoulder the credit or the blame that results.

An Oct. 30, 1996, editorial in The Huntsville Times describes newly elected
Mayor Spencer's ambitious reorganization plan for city government.

By January 1997 her cabinet was in place. She was the first mayor to hire a veterinarian to lead the Animal Services department and a director for Clean Community, which would later become Operation Green Team.

No matter how well equipped one is for a job, challenging circumstances will arise. In Mayor Spencer's case, one came quickly with the snow of Jan. 10, 1997.

A tremendous amount of snow fell quickly and froze quickly. Businesses let employees leave early after the snow had started to fall. That combination made for tumultuous conditions on the roads.

Mayor Spencer and several city employees were returning to Huntsville after reviewing a new jail design in Decatur, Ga. A truck jack-knifed at Governors Drive and Monte Sano Boulevard. The accident hindered a school bus taking students home. A group of city employees saw the situation and began helping students exit the bus to safety.

During an after-action analysis, Mayor Spencer and department heads scrutinized how the extreme snowfall was handled and made changes for future weather events.

The new mayor also faced many anticipated challenges involving roads and city spaces.

The Southern Bypass – and its potential benefits for Huntsville – had been a hot topic around town for years before Loretta became mayor. There were discussions of making it a toll road. The route would take it through the southern portion of Redstone Arsenal, and that added to the complexity of the situation. There were about as many bypass supporters as there were opponents.

Another challenge widely debated in the public sphere was the possibility of moving Panoply and Big Spring Jam out of Big Spring International Park. City department directors had suggested that the festivals be moved because of the negative impact large festivals had had on the landscape in previous years as well as anticipated construction in the park. Mayor Spencer said that she wanted to give the organizers plenty of time to adjust to any changes.

This plan was unpopular with a very vocal group. In 1997 Panoply had been held in Big Spring Park for 16 years and was an established tradition. Groups and individuals expressed their opinions and reviewed options for more than a week.

Panoply remains in Big Spring Park at the time of this writing in 2024. Big Spring Jam ended in the early 2000s as the national trend turned away from outdoor music festivals for a while. Weather played a significant role in the decision by disrupting the music festival for five consecutive years, placing the festival in the red.

The debate around the 1997 St. Patrick's Day parade is an example of a small but well-publicized challenge. Organizers sought to change the route to a difficult course, leaving from the southern portion of a heavily traveled road, Memorial Parkway South. Huntsville Police Department (HPD) advised against the course. However, like the issue of moving the two festivals, this one attracted a vocal group. Organizers even filed a request at the last minute for the previously unapproved route. HPD did not waiver on the previously denied route.

The parade moved to Madison after all the headaches. Post parade, The Huntsville Times described the event as "mayor bashing." It was an unfortunate situation, but the mayor is the person the public holds responsible when city decisions do not agree with their own.

Chapter Eleven

First-Term Accomplishments

N umerous accomplishments accompanied the challenges Mayor Spencer faced during her first term.

A report card article in The Huntsville Times on Oct. 19, 1997, gives City Council members "grades" for Mayor Spencer's first year in office. Always one to hold herself to a high standard, the mayor gave herself a B+ in her self-analysis, as did Councilman Bill Kling in his. These were the lowest grades given.

Among the many accomplishments mentioned in that article are the improved, open communication between the mayor and the City Council, economic development, lobbying for more state dollars for roads, property purchased for Research Park expansions, education improvements, and the transfer of Army jobs to Redstone Arsenal from St. Louis through the Base Realignment and Closure Act (BRAC) of 1995.

Huntsville's fiscal health was a challenge that became an accomplishment under Mayor Spencer's leadership. When she took office, the City of Huntsville was in debt – not a desired position for any city but especially not for one with high growth aspirations. Debt affects city services, economic development, and the stability of the municipality at its core.

She set a goal to cut costs while improving services in her first year. At the end of the fiscal year, the city had a $5 million carry-over. Department directors were on board with the mayor's plans, and she promised them that the carry-over money would be used to buy much-needed equipment.

Building a new 911 Center was another big success. The old center was located in the old downtown Huntsville-Madison County Public Library building at the corner of Fountain Circle and Williams Avenue. The new center was an advantageous partnership between Madison County, Huntsville and the City of Madison with a centralized setting that provided for better synergy between responding departments. Typical of her hands-on style, Mayor Spencer visited the 911 Center and listened in on calls so she would better understand the types of situations the responders were facing.

As of this writing, the 911 Center continues to provide Huntsville, Madison and Madison County with efficient coordination to better serve the public.

The new 911 Center was a partnership between Madison County, Huntsville and the City of Madison. Mayor Spencer visited the center and listened in on calls.

The City of Huntsville also enhanced its Emergency Management Agency operations. The decision was made to move the department out of the old jail building, which was later called the Municipal Complex Annex, located on Fountain Circle. There were many reasons to make this change, including the practical one that the prisoners had to be relocated to the basement of the Municipal Complex Annex each time there was a tornado warning. Mayor Spencer suggested that EMA move to a larger facility, and they chose the basement of the building where the Engineering and Inspection Departments were located.

Mayor Spencer put funding in the city's budget for the relocation, and the EMA staff did all the work themselves to save money. EMA's Operation Center was established and functioned better for all agencies. The center became the alternate location for the 911 Center if they became inoperable at their new location. All parties were very pleased with the excellent job done by the EMA staff.

Another big public safely step forward was the groundbreaking for a new Public Safety Complex on Wheeler Avenue to house the Municipal Court offices and courtrooms as well as Huntsville's Police Department and Municipal Jail.

A recap of Mayor Spencer's first year as recorded in The Huntsville Times on Oct. 20, 1997, gives these statistics: 31 ribbons cut for new businesses/companies, 21 visits to schools and 77 speeches given. The editorial board also wrote that, at many of the speaking engagements, Mayor Spencer was "often applauded before being introduced."

Chapter Twelve

Economic Development Deals

*M*ayor Spencer had become quite familiar with the path to successful economic development long before she took office. She had perfected a winning strategy based on her experience working in the formation of Cummings Research Park West combined with her years of recruiting industry as a volunteer by bringing the right people to the table. This proven method continued to yield good results during her years in office.

During her tenure, Huntsville became known as a stalwart of economic development with announcements occurring on a regular basis. Mayor Spencer credited this success to multiple factors, including a skilled workforce, good quality of life, and a welcoming community.

In 2002 Huntsville began appearing on numerous national rankings and listings of the best places to live. The city had applied for some of these but not the majority of them. Most were earned based on the ranking organizations' analysis of the city.

Recruiting new companies to locate in a city involves, to some extent, everyone in the city. That was Mayor Spencer's philosophy. She put her philosophy into action by telling people who worked in public service jobs – fast-food drive-thrus or other restaurants or retail stores – that they had an important role to play in helping the community land new jobs. The mayor had long been aware that company scouts visit cities to see what it is really like to live in an area. They ask questions and listen to conversations to get the real story.

Just a partial list of companies that have invested in Huntsville indicates the extent of the city's economic success story: ADTRAN, Ball

Aerospace, Boeing, Booz Allen Hamilton Inc., Digium, HudsonAlpha Institute for Biotechnology, Northrop Grumman, Raytheon, Sikorsky Aircraft Corporation, Sparta, Target Distribution Center, Torch Technologies, Verizon, and Yulista.

The dance of economic development has two paths, and Huntsville was in the enviable position to be able to evaluate companies interested in locating operations here. Recruiting quality companies pays dividends for many years. Mayor Spencer knew the importance of carefully selecting companies based on the long-term benefits they could bring to the community.

Toyota comes to town

Loretta Spencer's efforts helped seal the deal with many companies that chose to establish a presence in Huntsville and later expand operations. Toyota is a shining example.

Toyota Motor Manufacturing North America completed construction of its facility in the North Huntsville Industrial Park in 2003. Since the initial opening, the campus has successfully completed five expansions. Two expansions were within the first 14 months of operations. This is a testament to the company's success with the diverse workforce in the region. Each expansion brought more jobs and a quality workforce.

Mayor Spencer knew that Toyota locating a motor manufacturing plant in Huntsville could bring long-term benefits to the city and the region. Not only would Toyota bring good-paying jobs, but the company also is known for being a tremendous corporate citizen and enhancing a community through volunteering and investment.

"Toyota is a company that shares its success by supporting community needs," she said.

When Toyota established a presence in West Virginia, the company purchased a much-needed firetruck for that city. As their gift to Huntsville's community, they donated $500,000 to the Schools Foundation. Their generous gift provided the funding for a distance learning initiative for the area. Mayor Spencer's daughter, Sarah Spencer Chappell, was on the board of the Schools Foundation and knew the need for furthering education in surrounding communities.

Mayor Spencer laid the groundwork for Toyota's Huntsville presence well in advance of the facility's groundbreaking. Her Research Park experience had shown her that the right land was essential.

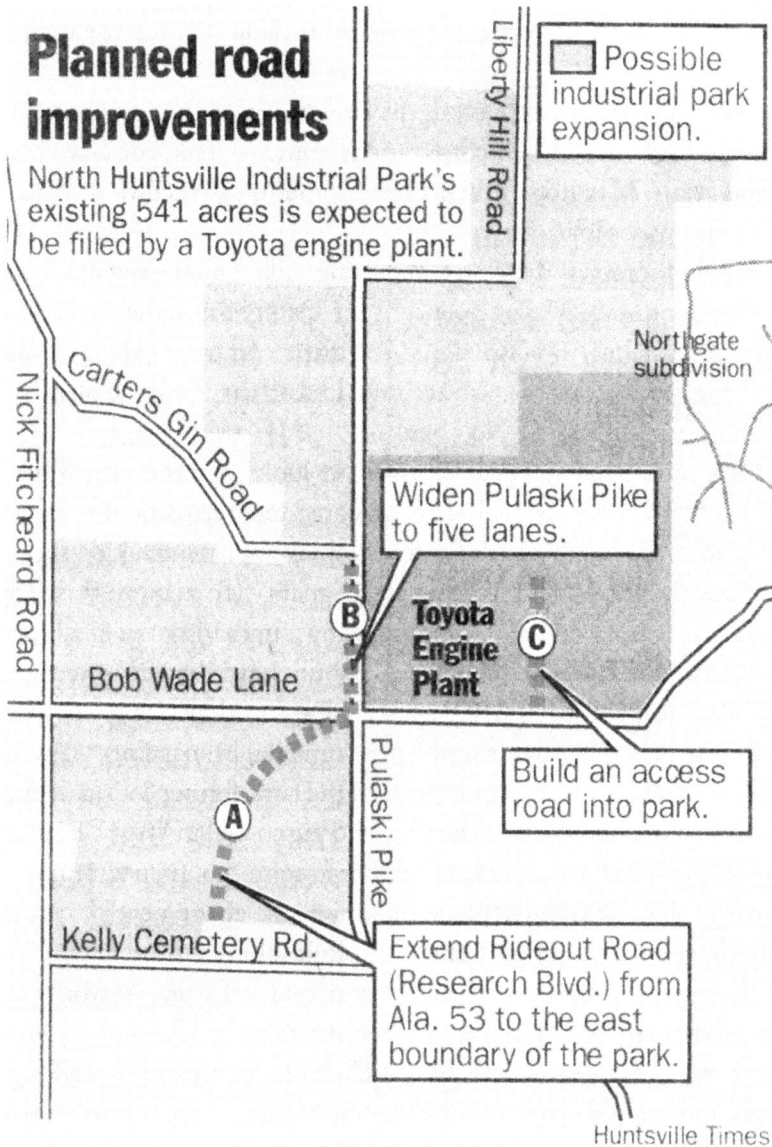

Planned road improvements

North Huntsville Industrial Park's existing 541 acres is expected to be filled by a Toyota engine plant.

Liberty Hill Road

☐ Possible industrial park expansion.

Nick Fitcheard Road

Carters Gin Road

Northgate subdivision

Widen Pulaski Pike to five lanes.

Ⓑ

Toyota Engine Plant Ⓒ

Bob Wade Lane

Build an access road into park.

Pulaski Pike

Ⓐ

Kelly Cemetery Rd.

Extend Rideout Road (Research Blvd.) from Ala. 53 to the east boundary of the park.

Huntsville Times

Planned road improvements to North Huntsville Industrial Park to prepare for the Toyota engine plant from The Huntsville Times.

The family that owned the land off Pulaski Pike, where Toyota Motor Manufacturing, Alabama, Inc. is now located, had moved out of state, and they were ready to sell the property. Other landowners in the area also became interested in selling. This resulted in a larger tract being available. The city purchased the land and made it ready for interested corporations.

"We made the investment in the land because it was always a factor," the mayor explains. "When corporations come to look, you have to have the land ready. It is important to have some infrastructure in place like utilities and water lines."

The first company interested in putting a plant on the site was involved in the food industry. Mayor Spencer sent Danny Shea, the city's director of natural resources, to Nashville to see if the company had any negative aspects. He quickly saw that ash accumulated on cars from the plant's stove pipes. So Huntsville said, "No, thanks."

One month later, Toyota arrived to look over the city. Since the opening of its facility, Toyota has been a consistent recipient of Huntsville's Air Pollution Control Awards for their achievements in making sure their operations do not negatively impact air quality. To achieve this, Toyota designed their plant to reduce emissions by eliminating the need for volatile organic compound chemicals. Not only have they been recognized for this by the City of Huntsville since 2004, but they also won an award from the Alabama Department of Environmental Management (ADEM).

Toyota officials were impressed that the land, former cotton fields, was flat and clear of boulders. The site they had purchased in West Virginia was not at all flat, extremely rocky, and required more site preparation.

More than 35,000 people applied for jobs at the new Toyota plant when it opened, backing up traffic from Pulaski Pike to Interstate 565.

To help provide enough skilled workers for Toyota, Mayor Spencer asked Alabama Industrial Development Training (AIDT) to provide training at J.F. Drake State Technical College. Along with benefiting the workers and the company, this agreement enhanced the training capabilities at Drake.

Toyota initially committed to hiring 250 employees. The number of jobs has steadily increased since operations began. Toyota's reputation

Toyota Motor Corporation President Fujio Cho shakes the hand of Alabama Gov. Don Siegelman over a V8 engine this morning.

Toyota to build $230 million plant here

Toyota plant announcement in The Huntsville Times.

as a good company to work for, with opportunities to train and advance, enhances the expansions. People want to work for good companies.

The Toyota deal did have its challenges, Mayor Spencer notes. This was an exciting development for Huntsville and the region, but Toyota had asked that the city keep the news under wraps until the following February. The company always shuts down for two weeks during the holidays, and officials wanted to time the announcement around that break.

During this "hush" time, a group of ladies from north Huntsville asked during a meeting about the development being done in their area. A City Council member let the secret slip, breaking the agreement with Toyota. The problem was worked out, as evidenced by the history of the company here. However, it did add a somewhat rocky start to the relationship.

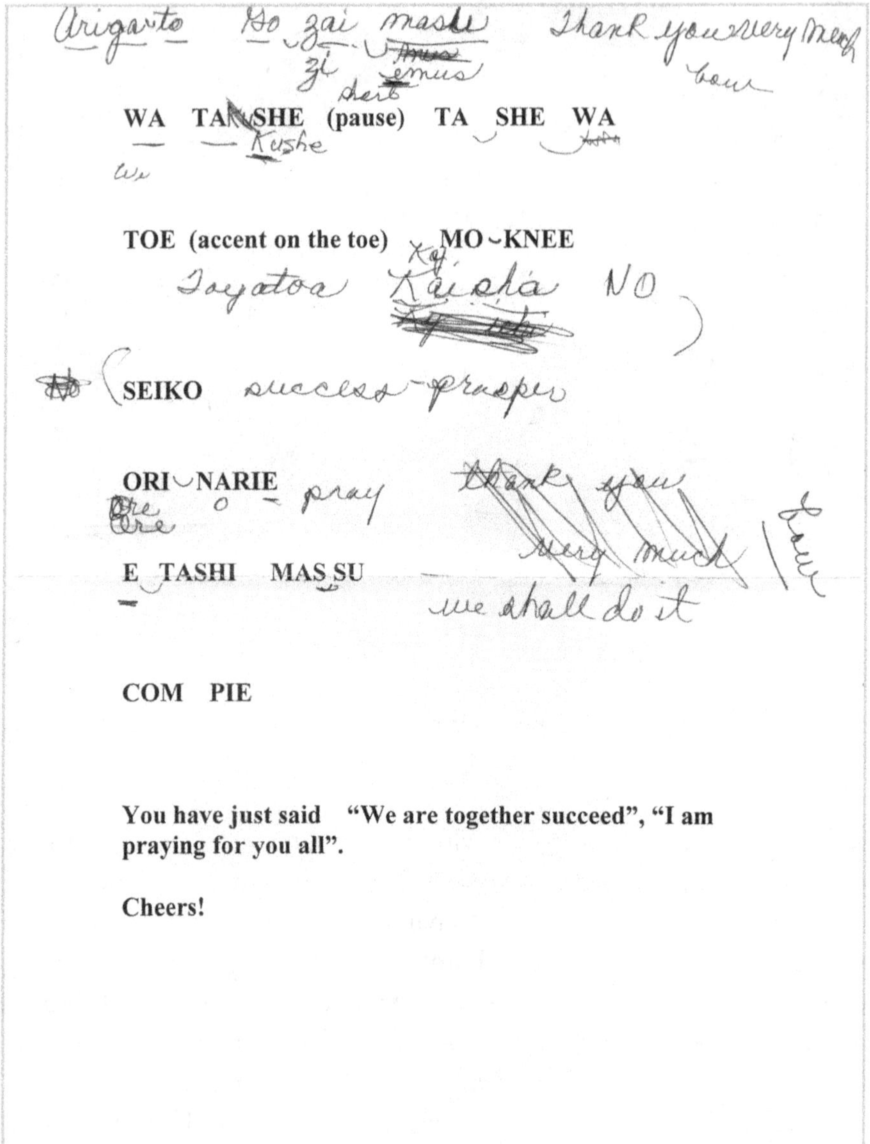

Arigarto   Go zai maste   Thank you very much
            zi   emus   bow
            dert

WA TA SHE (pause) TA SHE WA
            Kushe
Wa

TOE (accent on the toe)   MO~KNEE

Toyota   Kaisla   NO

(SEIKO   success prosper

ORI~NARIE   pray   thank you
ore   o
are   very much   bow

E TASHI MAS SU
                    we shall do it

COM   PIE

You have just said   "We are together succeed", "I am
praying for you all".

Cheers!

Mayor Spencer's comments in Japanese to welcome the Toyota delegation.

Janice Fowler, Mayor Spencer and Barbara McDaniel

One of the many positive relationships that came from the Toyota development involved Barbara McDaniel, the manager of external affairs for Toyota Motor Manufacturing, Inc. of North America. She would often drive from Kentucky to Huntsville and kept communication open, giving suggestions on how the city could be a better partner as well as offer Toyota's assistance to organizations in the area to support those aligned with Toyota's goals. One time Barbara asked if they could request that the Marriott repair a damaged table frequently used during their meetings with another group from Toyota. The Marriott had the problem fixed well before the next meeting. Through working together, Barbara, Mayor Spencer and Janice Fowler, the mayor's assistant, became close friends for life. This is a prime example of how relationships continue long after investments are made.

Expanding on Toyota's success in Huntsville, Toyota and Mazda announced in 2018 that the two companies would build a joint-venture assembly plant in Huntsville. The $1.6 billion plant would bring

4,000 new jobs to the region with an average annual salary of $50,000, according to CNN Money, Jan. 10, 2018.

The site of Mazda Toyota Manufacturing USA, Inc. is the parcel of land that had been targeted for a Volkswagen plant. In 2008 Huntsville was one of the two final locations considered for Volkswagen's manufacturing facility that ended up going to Chattanooga.

City officials knew that this location with its proximity to the interstate would be attractive to corporations. Having the actual site ready was only one part of the preplanning for recruitment. There would need to be plans for residential development as well as city services such as sewer and an additional fire station in the area.

With more companies locating in the western part of Huntsville, another important feature would be schools to serve the families that would move to the area. The Albert McDonald family generously donated land for an elementary school to be built and provided additional land at a discounted price for a middle school.

Families usually want to live in areas close to schools and work. Albert and Shirley McDonald were very interested in helping Huntsville's efforts to expand and bring more jobs to the area. Their vision and willingness to provide the land is paying dividends to Huntsville and the surrounding counties now and will likely continue to do so for many years to come.

Chapter Thirteen

Storefront Economic Development

$\mathcal{H}$aving well-paying jobs is one vital piece of a city's economic development puzzle. Having attractive retail offerings is just as essential to assembling the whole picture. If a city does not have the shopping options its residents want, then they'll spend their discretionary income elsewhere. Alabama cities are funded by sales tax, and Mayor Spencer was eager to expand Huntsville's storefronts and grow that tax base.

Parkway City to Parkway Place

One of her first big retail projects was revitalizing Parkway City Mall at Drake Avenue and Memorial Parkway. The mall first opened in 1957 as Parkway Shopping Center, a strip mall with 25 stores. After a tornado destroyed the south end of the center on April 3, 1974, the complex was renovated as a single-level enclosed mall which reopened in February 1976 with Parisian, Pizitz and Montgomery Ward as anchors. It was Huntsville's largest shopping center until Madison Square Mall opened in 1984. By the time Mayor Spencer was in office, the aging Parkway City was losing stores and businesses.

Huntsville had a proven ability to support retail, and Mayor Spencer viewed Parkway City Mall as a challenge and an opportunity. Plans to redevelop the location began in 1998 and involved a lot of moving parts – and stores.

One of Parkway City's anchors was Parisian, a popular department store chain then headquartered in Alabama, and it remained in operation throughout the redevelopment. Parisian bought Montgomery Ward's former location on the north end of the mall, demolished it, and then built a two-story building. Not only did Parisian sustain operations as a standalone store for one year, it thrived as the second-highest performing Parisian store in its division. With the headaches and hurdles of construction, this was no small feat.

Parisian's success gratified Mayor Spencer personally as well as professionally. She recalled when Decatur had a Parisian store before one located in Huntsville. Huntsville had been held back for years due to lack of access to the interstate. By the time Interstate 565 was fully open in December 1991, it had taken more than 20 years to construct this connection from I-65 to U.S. 72 in Huntsville. I-565 provided corporations with a more efficient way to transport goods, making it easier to persuade them to locate and expand in Huntsville. The interstate spur also facilitated workers' commutes.

Parisian was an important corner piece of the new mall's picture. To assemble the rest of the puzzle, Mayor Spencer invited Michael Lebovitz, president of CBL, Inc. to come to Huntsville. She wanted to gauge his interest in building a new mall at the Parkway City location to connect to Parisian. She arranged a visit to the site and lunch at Clementine's on Madison Street, and the deal was in motion. The mayor agreed that the City of Huntsville would partner on the cost of the mall's parking garage.

(If you asked Loretta's brother, John, he might tell you this deal-making scenario reminded him of her negotiations to share the costs of gifts and other treats with him when they were children.)

CBL had built the newer Madison Square Mall in the mid-1980s when Loretta was chairman of the Planning Commission. She had worked with Lebovitz's cousin on that project. CBL was continuing to build shopping centers and had at least 50 across the country.

CBL recognized that this was a valuable shopping center to Huntsville. Mayor Spencer knew a new mall would provide a substantial amount of sales tax dollars for the city. She persuaded the City Council to approve a Tax Increment Financing District, which provided money

Mayor Spencer takes part in the grand opening events
for the new Parkway Place Mall.

to build a new Huntsville High School building on Bob Wallace Avenue close by the mall.

Part of the negotiation with CBL involved the developer recruiting Williams Sonoma, Carrabba's and another upscale department store to anchor one end of the mall. Castner Knott was the original tenant on one end with Parisian on the other. As of this writing, Dillard's has replaced Castner Knott, and Belk has replaced Parisian. An elevator from Japan was the first feature of Castner Knott's location, and it had to be installed before the building was built.

Village of Providence

Mayor Spencer was a keen observer of changes in the shopping climate, and she recognized that retail needed to be combined with destination places offering a variety of shops, restaurants, attractions, hotels, and residential and office spaces.

The first of these multi-use live, work, play projects was the Village of Providence Town Center. The idyllic setting, tucked not too far from a major corridor, combined upscale housing with walkability to restaurants and shops. Mayor Spencer kept her strong focus on education during the negotiations for the development, and she insisted that they build a new school.

Brothers Todd Slyman and David Slyman developed the now very popular Providence area. Many meetings and public queries were held prior to the development. The brothers held charrettes to show development concepts and gather input from interested businesses and individuals.

Grille 29 was one of the first restaurants. The Slymans knew from their travels, especially in the Orlando area, that this classic restaurant would do well in Huntsville. Grille 29 flew in a pastry chef for the announcement of the development, and attendees at the announcement were impressed – a sign of good things to come.

Constructing a bridge was another proactive step taken to prepare the development for growth. However, the project drew political fire from many. Some people didn't understand the need to spend $1 million. Mayor Spencer knew the bridge was necessary because it addressed drainage issues in the area connected to Indian Creek, and it was the link to high-end houses in the development for continuation of the project.

Furthermore, U.S. Rep. Bud Cramer found the money to build it.

"Sometimes you have to capitalize on an opportunity when money is available," Mayor Spencer said. "Funny how the bridge isn't questioned today."

Crossing Bridge Street

Bridge Street Town Centre, which officially opened in November 2007, was another take on this type of development. Huntsville worked with O&S Holdings, owned by Paul Orfalea and Gary Safady. They showed interest in 2002 to develop this now extremely popular shopping, dining and entertainment destination.

Knowing that establishing good relationships is key to success, Mayor Spencer personally gifted Space Camp experiences to two of Safady's children. In turn he delivered on the requests by residents for features and retail in the outdoor venture. They reached an agreement by December 2002.

When Mayor Spencer came into office, she and Safady agreed that they would have an understanding – a "can-do" attitude. The developers were a group from California where the construction practices were completely different from Alabama standards.

This project was at times a painstaking one. Hulan Smith, director of the city's Inspection Department, had to review two sets of plans due to the many changes to the project. Hulan was one of the most respected inspectors in the state and a great friend to the mayor. His work ethic and attention to detail helped Bridge Street become a reality.

Within this development was the first Westin, a five-star hotel, to be located in Alabama. The hotel opened in the summer of 2008.

Mayor Spencer asked the community which stores and restaurants were on their wish list. P.F. Chang's was at the top, so the trademark majestic stone horses were part of the official opening's popular photo stops. Mayor Spencer mentioned that "P.F. Chang's was definitely on my list."

Monaco Pictures, a movie theater specializing in the total experience with reserved-seat ticketing, VIP areas for adults, wine tasting stations and a trendy restaurant with indoor and outdoor dining, was an immediate success.

Anyone who attended the initial openings of Bridge Street Town Centre, Monaco Pictures or the Westin will tell you they were indeed grand and red-carpet worthy. In fact, guests of the invitation-only opening of Monaco Pictures walked on roped-off red carpet from the parking area into the theater's entrance.

Coincidentally, P.F. Chang's figured into another Bridge Street negotiation that did not pan out. When the outdoor shopping concept in Huntsville was first being discussed, Mayor Spencer met with Bayer Properties, the owners of The Summit in Birmingham, to gauge their interest in doing a project in Huntsville. They invited her to go to Birmingham for a meeting, and they took her to P.F. Chang's.

At that time Bayer Properties had three other projects in Colorado, West Virginia and Kentucky in process, so the timing would not work. They proposed that they could complete the Huntsville project in three years. O&S Holdings indicated in their proposal that they could complete it in two years. It ended up taking them at least three years. Things have a way of coming full circle though. O&S Holdings sold Bridge Street within four years of its opening. For several years, Bayer Properties owned and managed Bridge Street. Tanger Inc. acquired Bridge Street in late 2023.

Some people will remember what Old Madison Pike looked like before the Bridge Street development. It was farmland owned by the McDonald family. The farmland bordered the developing Cummings Research Park West. Mayor Spencer tells this story about how the property was acquired:

> *We needed a 500-acre site for the multi-use development. I had been saving the property to add places that would provide needs for the people working in CRP West. We knew that employees working in the park would need places to grab a quick lunch, post office, pharmacy and a dry cleaner. High on the list also were day care facilities that would be close by.*

The land that had been reserved for the multi-use facility was sold to Mark Smith for ADTRAN's expansion. Smith requested a meeting to see if he could buy an additional tract of land. He had invested in CRP West significantly already. ADTRAN's success and the number of additional jobs its expansion would provide were enough to decide that it made sense to sell that land for ADTRAN's second building.

Then the great opportunities began to come. The sale of that land provided the funds needed to acquire the McDonald Farm, which bordered CRP West with Old Madison Pike on the southern side and Research Park Boulevard on the eastern edge. Not to mention, it was easily accessible from I-565. The connectivity was there to provide easy access not only to people working in CRP West, but also Redstone Arsenal.

Building Bridge Street Town Centre was not an easy process, but it was worth the time and patience. Bridge Street is an asset to Huntsville. O&S Holdings built Bridge Street, and Bayer Properties is continuing the plan by adding residences and additional retail and restaurant businesses.

Target Distribution Center

Reviewing the timeline for developments during Mayor Spencer's administration shows consistent and frequent announcements, and each one was well planned to expand and build the city methodically. The Target Distribution Center in the western part of the city was another milestone retail development put in place just before the Toyota Motor Manufacturing facility.

The Target Center provides desirable full-time and seasonal jobs and the distinction of Huntsville being home to a distribution center of a major retailer. The center not only affects the Tennessee Valley region, it serves five states.

Mayor Spencer remembers her impression of the scope of the distribution center's operations when 19 Target employees drove her around in a golf cart to see the facility. They covered the area equivalent to 14 football fields. Seeing Target trucks on the road today reminds her of the project's success. She's also proud of the fact that the facility's manager, originally scheduled to be in Huntsville for only two years, chose to remain in the city, evidence of the community's high quality of life that had been established.

The Target Distribution Center was a great example of Huntsville working with state and federal entities quickly to put a deal together.

*Mayor Spencer, far left, marks the Target Distribution Center project
with Target officials as well as Alabama Gov. Don Siegelman,
third from right, and U.S. Rep. Bud Cramer, far right.*

Mayor Spencer had just returned from meetings in Washington, D.C. She talked with Target's headquarters in Minneapolis at 9 a.m. on a Friday to find out the difference in proposals and about Huntsville's competition. They called her back at 11 a.m.: To successfully recruit the 1,357,500-square-foot distribution center, Huntsville would have to have $750,000 secured by the following Monday morning.

The city and the mayor were on a tight deadline. She would have to recruit as much assistance as possible, as quickly as possible.

Mayor Spencer called the office of then-Gov. Don Siegelman around noon, but the people she needed to talk to were out of the office attending car races at Talladega. She was able to get in touch with the governor, who was with the state's industrial development director. Her persistence paid off, and Siegelman committed $250,000 to the project on the spot.

Target's economic boost

■ Getting a Dayton Hudson warehouse and distribution center to Huntsville is a major coup for North Alabama.

Take a 154-acre parcel of prime Huntsville land next to I-565 and a cooperative effort among the state of Alabama, U.S. Rep. Bud Cramer, Tennessee Valley Authority Chairman Craven Crowell, Huntsville Mayor Loretta Spencer, the Huntsville/Madison County Chamber of Commerce and the Limestone County Industrial Development Association. Add to it a national corporation looking for a location to build a multi-million dollar facility.

What do you get? A project that's right on Target.

The Minneapolis-based Dayton Hudson Corp., owner of the chain of Target stores, will be building a warehouse and distribution center here — at the interchange of I-565 and Greenbrier Road — that will probably employ 800 workers by 2004. The 1.2-million square-foot facility will cost $60 million to $80 million.

All these numbers add up to a welcome boon to North Alabama.

A hush-hush deal for several weeks, the location of the center may eventually lead to something else that officials are being careful in talking about: a couple

Accolades

of Target stores. No one will even speculate about it on the record, but it's clear that in order for the center's employees to take full advantage of their benefits package, they will need to have access to at least one Target store. Target employees can shop at the stores at a discount.

Certainly, it makes eminent sense to locate Target stores near the distribution center to take advantage of favorable transportation costs. Huntsville's retail mix could use another player; Huntsville's tax base could use it, too.

Regardless of whether Target locates one or more stores here, it's clear that the center adds heft to North Alabama's economy. Even Gov. Don Siegelman made the trip north from Montgomery for the announcement.

In his remarks, Siegelman proclaimed that the days when quality jobs pass Alabama by are over. He seems to be right.

We certainly hope he is. Quality jobs add to our quality of life.

And for far too long, Alabama has been lagging behind most of the other 49 states in that department. We applaud state and local officials for working together to make Huntsville and Madison and Limestone Counties an irresistible choice.

The Target Distribution Center was a big win for Huntsville,
as this editorial from The Huntsville Times points out.

For help in obtaining the rest of the funding, Mayor Spencer called U.S. Rep. Bud Cramer, who was at the airport in D.C. on his way back to Huntsville. She asked Cramer to contact Glenn McCullough, Jr. from Mississippi, who was chair of the Tennessee Valley Authority (TVA) board. Bill Pippen, CEO of Huntsville Utilities at that time, had made the mayor aware of two levels of loans from TVA. Also, Pippen had always included her in discussions, so she had met and talked with McCullough many times.

Cramer immediately contacted McCullough and asked for TVA to contribute the remaining $500,000. When McCullough replied that he would need time to think about it, Cramer said that he could think about it all he wanted, but they needed an answer before 5 p.m. that day.

Normally, city department heads might like to leave a bit early on a Friday afternoon, especially after a long City Council meeting the night before. Not this time. There was too much on the line.

Cramer called back by 5 p.m. with the answer. TVA would provide $500,000, and Mayor Spencer had a Target deal.

In a Chamber of Commerce announcement of the project, Target CEO Bob Ulrich said he never thought that Mayor Spencer would be able to pull it off in such a short timeframe. Needless to say, he had not known the mayor for very long and was not yet aware of the ability of the city to adapt and meet its goals.

Cracker Barrel

Huntsville, with the leadership of Mayor Spencer, had the Midas touch for retail with record-setting company openings and sales.

Cracker Barrel opened its first Old Country Store that was located within a city, not off an interstate, in Huntsville. The company had been interested in the location at Drake Avenue and Memorial Parkway for some time. As he had done with other projects, Inspection Department Director Hulan Smith played a major role in making this investment go smoothly. He knew that Cracker Barrel had been making inquiries about the location; however, at that time the site was a bit of an eyesore. The right business occupying that space could turn it into a successful part of the city's economic landscape.

Cracker Barrel opened two other locations on interstates on the same day that they opened the restaurant in Huntsville. The Huntsville opening well outperformed the others, and this location continued to break all company records for sales on a regular basis.

At company headquarters, located not too far away in Franklin, Tenn., they noticed what was happening in Huntsville. The success was so noteworthy that Cracker Barrel responded within a week to the idea of placing three new restaurants in Huntsville in 2008 by sending their senior vice president of real estate to meet with Mayor Spencer. The deal was almost done, but then a leadership change in the city and an unstable national economy later in 2008 altered the prospects, and the deal was over.

Embassy Suites

Mayor Spencer always emphasized the importance of establishing good relationships and fulfilling your promises. In the case of Embassy Suites coming to Huntsville, both became paramount.

John Q. Hammons was a billionaire tycoon in the lodging and hospitality industry who passed away in 2013. His life and success story are chronicled in his biography, *They Call Him John Q: A Hotel Legend*. He was considering building a hotel in Huntsville in the mid-1990s, but the City of Huntsville did not fulfill its commitment to him in 1994 and pulled out of the deal at the last minute.

Mr. Hammons already had plans designed for the hotel. The site work had not been done, but the investment had been made in design work. He sued the city for $500,000 and won. That was his first experience with Huntsville. Instead of Huntsville, Mr. Hammons built the hotel in Montgomery by the Alabama River.

It was Huntsville's loss, but that loss proved to be only temporary.

Mr. Hammons' first impression of Huntsville was not a good one, but he was willing to come back to the table and talk with a new mayor and City Council in 2003.

Mayor Spencer invited him to her home. He told her that he had never been invited to a mayor's home. Surrounded by City Finance Director

Randy Taylor and members from the city's legal and planning departments, they talked about their vision for Huntsville, growth of conventions at the VBC, and strengthening the downtown core.

A homemade lunch of chicken salad and fruit salad with chocolates for dessert – plus notes on a napkin – formed the beginnings of a great friendship and a $40 million investment in Huntsville.

Wednesday turned out to be a significant day in the story of Embassy Suites coming to Huntsville as Mayor Spencer and Mr. Hammons met on three consecutive Wednesdays.

At their first meeting, the mayor said the hotel needed to have 250 rooms. The next week Mr. Hammons asked how she felt about 300 rooms.

Mayor Spencer requested a Ruth's Chris Steak House in the hotel. Mr. Hammons said he would have to build a second kitchen. During their discussion, she reminded him that he could rent out floor space, and they agreed that the hotel would rent space to the restaurant. This was during a time period when Huntsville was recruiting the top restaurants.

When Mr. Hammons asked the mayor in June before the November opening if she wanted the hotel to have a spa, she had a few questions, including, "How much will it cost?" His reply: three hotel rooms. Knowing this would be a great amenity for people staying at the hotel, she said it was a deal.

With a new perspective of Huntsville, Mr. Hammons returned to the city and built Embassy Suites – with a Ruth's Chris Steak House and a spa. The hotel opened in November 2006, and it's still paying dividends to the city's tourism and convention industry.

Mayor Spencer and her team had re-established trust with Mr. Hammons, and of his more than 200 hotels in 40 states, Huntsville's was the top performer. Because of the value he now placed on Huntsville, he insisted on this location's premiere suite to be named the "Mayor's Suite" instead of the traditional "Presidential Suite."

The mayor and the developer each had great trust in the other to see that this project would be a positive one for Huntsville. After a meeting with The Huntsville Times' Editorial Board to make the announcement, Mayor Spencer said, "I shake hands on new business deals, but I hug on

Mike Mercier/Huntsville Times

Embassy Suites front office manager Serena Lotz, left, checks in Mayor Loretta Spencer as the hotel's first official guest Tuesday.

*After working so hard to get an Embassy Suites hotel in Huntsville,
Mayor Spencer became its first official guest.*

new friendships." Her remark stuck with the savvy businessman. Sometime later, he called her office to inform her that today was a "Hug Day." He told her he was in Oklahoma City, and they had a female mayor too.

Mayor Spencer would send Mr. Hammons inexpensive "loud ties," which he favored, for his birthday. He would send her flowers for Mother's Day and remember her on other special occasions.

The trust they had in doing business and the success of the location in Huntsville led Mr. Hammons to plan to build another hotel in Huntsville. He had also committed to building a Conference Hotel if the Volkswagen plant, unfortunately lost to Chattanooga, had located in Huntsville. However, due to Mr. Hammons' declining health and changing times, a second hotel did not happen.

Huntsville made a lasting impression on the owners/investors of Ruth's Chris Steak House during their opening weekend because there was so much excitement and fun. The first night featured a table for eight designated "The Mayor's Table." Mayor Spencer used this quite often during her term and afterwards for special guests to Huntsville. Nancy Oswald, one of the owners and the owner of the largest Ruth's Chris franchise, asked Mayor Spencer to lead a parade around the dining room. Of course, the mayor joined in on this tradition. One of the partners was the original accountant for Mrs. Ruth in New Orleans and had so many stories of fond memories of Mrs. Ruth.

It quickly became evident that the investors wanted to help organizations in Huntsville. They decided to hold a fundraiser during their opening for the National Children's Advocacy Center (NCAC), located in Huntsville. Proceeds from bottles of wine selling for $100 each were donated to the organization. Congressman Cramer was invited to attend and enjoy the festivities, including a jazz band brought in from New Orleans. Cramer had founded the NCAC while he was the district attorney for Madison County after seeing the need for a better system to handle child abuse cases.

Mayor Spencer, third from left, joins area officials at the groundbreaking
for the future home of the National Children's Advocacy Center.
She's standing next to U.S. Rep. Bud Cramer, who founded the organization.

Mayor Spencer and Huntsville's General Services Director Jeff Easter had been evaluating several city operating facilities. The more they looked into the situation, the more convinced they became that the best route for the city and the NCAC would be to close the department's location where the present NCAC campus is located. That would give the organization a visible and easily accessible site. Cecil Ashburn sold adjoining land at a discount to provide ample area for the campus. The existing gym owned by the city was in really good shape and could be used by NCAC. The city department moved to Washington Street where more area was available for equipment and vehicles.

During the opening of the NCAC's new location, the actress Jane Seymour came to speak at the event. She donated holiday ornaments, designed by her, to be sold during the benefit as well as the next day at Parisian, where she autographed each one purchased.

Mayor Spencer met Jane Seymour when the actress came to Huntsville for a fundraiser to benefit the National Children's Advocacy Center.

Huntsville has been fortunate to attract businesses, corporations and individuals who are willing to invest in so many ways to enhance the area's quality of life.

Decades earlier, all eyes had been on Decatur to be the anchor of the northern portion of Alabama. However, through successive leadership, Huntsville positioned itself to be a city that could build on success and continue to lead efforts benefiting and giving a boost to the North Alabama/ Tennessee Valley region.

Chapter Fourteen

Tax-Increment Financing Districts

*L*oretta Spencer's top commitments during her first mayoral campaign were road improvements, economic development (including retail) and schools. She wanted to raise the quality of life for people already living in Huntsville as well as attract new residents. To maintain Huntsville as a regional draw for tax dollars, Mayor Spencer and her team realized that they had to stay ahead of other areas to offer a variety of shopping choices. They used Tax Increment Financing Districts to make the city more competitive by building the infrastructure that would attract popular retail options.

TIFs allow municipalities to use projected revenue from future funding to stimulate economic development without raising tax rates. This is a simple description of a complex tool that Huntsville mastered during Mayor Spencer's administration. The major goal was to help the education system with property taxes earmarked for schools.

Mayor Spencer began this effort in 2002 with TIF 1, which became a highly successful tool for developing infrastructure needed to expand and grow retail along U.S. Highway 72 West. Integral to this plan was expanding U.S. 72 to seven lanes and securing the first Target location for Huntsville.

During her second year in office, Mayor Spencer was extremely selective when it came to choosing Randy Taylor as the city's finance director. His expertise would be vital in many areas. In regard to the TIFs, his projections were instrumental.

TIF 1 projections were extremely conservative for what turned out to be an enormously successful project, Westside Center, located close to Cummings Research Park. The debt was repaid nine years earlier than anticipated.

The city's first SuperTarget Center anchored the center. This development paved the way for the later Walmart Center project on U.S. 72 West near Balch Road which was conceived and negotiated in 2008.

The TIF success story

Huntsville officials took a fiscal risk, and that risk is paying off

In a football game, when a team, jumps out to a three-touchdown lead in the first quarter, it can still lose — but the chances of it losing are a lot less than if the game were tied after the first 15 minutes.

The City of Huntsville finds itself in much the same situation. Its tax increment financing districts, which use public infrastructure improvements to spur commercial development and thus generate higher property taxes, have jumped out to a commanding lead.

Last year, the property tax collections from the four districts together were $1.35 million, some 25 percent above projections, despite the national economic downturn.

And the increases are expected to continue. After 2009, the city will not have to lend itself money to pay back the principal and interest on the money it borrowed for the improvements. By that time, revenues from the districts will more than cover the city's expense.

And these are just the property taxes. The city's revenue to back pay the cost does not include sales taxes from the stores or the indirect effect of new businesses hiring people to work in the stores. All that's gravy. It goes into the city's general fund and city schools.

Again, the game is not over. It has, in some cases, 28 more years. But there's no reason to think the trend will reverse itself.

The purposes of the tax increments was twofold: to increase city revenues from undeveloped property that was generating little in taxes or from property whose value had drastically declined. The city, in turn, would enjoy the indirect benefits of the TIFs: rejuvenated portions of the city and development that would come into Huntsville rather than into Madison or other areas of Madison County.

City officials back in 2000 easily acknowledged the risk. But they also understood the necessity of taking positive action. The city, like many others, has an aging population. Young families were looking to Madison and Madison County because those school systems have new schools, and the new schools are near new homes.

The TIFs have enabled Huntsville to compete. Ground has been broken for a new Huntsville High next to the existing school. New schools will be located in west Huntsville, and developers plan to build subdivisions around those schools. Additional TIFs could lead to more schools and more new businesses generating property taxes.

Huntsville's successful utilization of the state law allowing TIFs is instructive in another way, as well. It illustrates the fact that the changing dynamics of the economy and demand constantly changing economic development strategies.

Fifty years ago, Huntsville embraced defense and aerospace spending because its economy depended heavily on those sectors. Later, it encouraged spin-off firms as well as companies engaged in the manufacture of hard goods unrelated to space and defense.

Then, when the economy shifted from one that *made* things to one that *did* things, Huntsville was able to land software and consulting firms, some home grown, some coming from elsewhere.

Today, the TIFs represent an integrated, multilevel approach. Much of the credit must go to Mayor Loretta Spencer and her staff, to the City Council, which was willing to take the risk, and to the County Commission, whose members generally voted for economic development despite their concerns.

Over time, things may change. An evolving economy can bring changes to the tax base. Internet sales are growing daily, and either local and state governments will have to find a way to tax such sales, or they will have to turn to other sources of revenue.

On the TIFs, the people with their necks on the line took a risk, and it's paying off handsomely. 2-10-03

Editorial from The Huntsville Times, Feb. 10, 2003, about the success of Mayor Spencer's tax increment financing districts.

The success of TIF 1 made it easier to get the next TIF approved.

TIF 2 focused on the city core. A new Huntsville High School was built through $10 million provided by the TIF, and a new parking garage for Parkway Place Mall was funded for $5.5 million. The new parking deck was part of the agreement with CBL Development to build Parkway Place Mall. The parking deck is well used today, especially on rainy or extremely hot days. While some people criticized it for being on the Memorial Parkway side of the mall, residents of the neighborhoods behind the mall expressed gratitude not only for the newly built mall but also the lack of a direct view of the two-story deck.

TIF 3 built two new schools by funding $30 million for Providence K-8 School and Columbia High School. In order to capitalize on building the new school, city employees did the site work on Providence K-8, making it possible to build seven additional classrooms. This was a major part of the deal to get the Providence project – a unique opportunity for Huntsville.

According to the City of Huntsville website, the TIF 3 debt was repaid 11 years ahead of schedule, and "the City returned $2.2 million to Huntsville City Schools, $1.2 million to the Madison County Commission, and $1.5 million to City operating and capital funds. Beginning in 2013, Huntsville City Schools will start receiving $4.7 million, Madison County Commission $2.8 million, and the City $3.2 million each year from property taxes formerly in the TIF." (Source: City of Huntsville website https://www.huntsvilleal.gov/government/finances-budget/tax-increment-financing-tif-districts/).

TIF 3A, as reported by The Decatur Daily on March 15, 2006, "provided $12 million for renovating eight northwest schools, $8 million for road improvements, $5.3 million for improvements to the North Huntsville Industrial Park to lure the Toyota engine plant, and $470,000 for other city facilities."

TIF 4 was the final TIF implemented during Mayor Spencer's administration. This TIF District included the city's downtown core. A new Lee High School was built with $13 million. The TIF also funded a new Public Safety Complex, combining police and fire operations, and provided improvements to the Huntsville Museum of Art and the Von Braun Center to remodel the Concert Hall and the Arena. The city combined TIF funds with the generous commitments of the Mark C. Smith Family for the Concert Hall and the Propst Family for the Arena to expand and upgrade these VBC venues, making them even stronger attractions on Huntsville's entertainment and convention scene.

TIF DISTRICT TAX COLLECTIONS
FISCAL YEAR 2009

1. TIF collections, compared to projections are:

	This Year	All Years
TIF 2	30.5%	23.2%
TIF 3	163.0%	112.4%
TIF 3A	20.9%	22.1%
TIF 4	8.7%	-22.5%

2. *TIF 3 HAS ACCUMULATED A $16 MILLION RESERVE TO PAY OFF DEBT EARLY.*

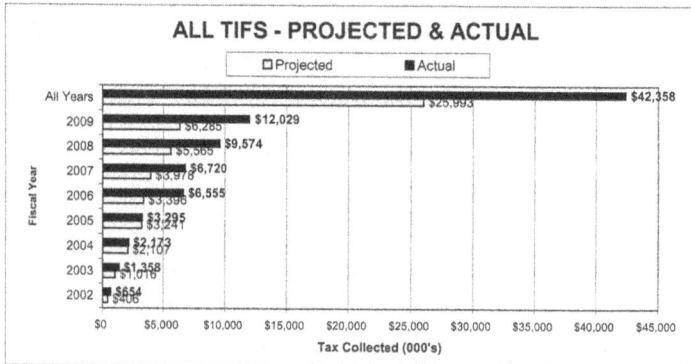

ALL TIFS - PROJECTED & ACTUAL

□ Projected   ■ Actual

Fiscal Year	Projected	Actual
All Years	$25,993	$42,358
2009	$6,285	$12,029
2008	$5,565	$9,574
2007	$3,978	$6,720
2006	$3,396	$6,555
2005	$3,241	$3,295
2004	$2,107	$2,773
2003	$1,019	$1,358
2002	$406	$654

Tax Collected (000's)

TIFs BENEFIT LOCAL SCHOOL SYSTEMS DIRECTLY

The 5.5 mill county-wide school tax is not part of the TIFs.
All growth caused by the TIFs has increased the 5.5 tax payment

From 2002 to 2009, TIFs increased tax payments to the school systems:

Huntsville City Schools	$4,509,746
Madison County Schools	$3,476,263
Madison City Schools	$1,409,296
Total	$9,395,304

The City of Huntsville, Madison County Commission, Madison County
Board of Education, and Madison City Schools also receive
DIRECT payments of new property tax money due to growth caused by TIFs,
BUT not included in the TIFs

9/27/2008   _ALL TIFS Collections - Summary Data.xls - CHARTS

TIF charts 1

The fifth TIF was initiated during Mayor Spencer's third term. This TIF committed to financing the new road to Redstone's airport as well as helping to develop the Enhanced Use Lease, which includes multiple spaces to eat and shop as well as a hotel.

Mayor Spencer's confidence in the city's ability to perform at a higher level paid off with the TIFs. Even at the time of this publication, the TIFs continue to pump additional money into city coffers, making more improvement projects possible.

When considering the number of schools built and the other funding provided to the school system, the impact of the TIFs on education is profound. This new money was over and beyond the portion of sale tax revenue that the city provides to the school system.

Chapter Fifteen

Building a Strong, Safe Quality of Life

The phrase "quality of life" can mean many things to different people. Mayor Spencer realized that the city had to make sure the basics are covered as well as incorporate extra amenities that can make a world of difference in attracting businesses and residents. Even before she became mayor, during her Planning Commission days, she approached the task with her typical level of organization and personal connections by putting people in a room to discuss quality of life issues and ways to improve them in the city of Huntsville.

During 1990-95, Loretta hosted focus groups monthly at The Heritage Club, a downtown private restaurant that was a popular destination for business meetings. The club's Library Room served as a great location for small group meetings to have privacy. On numerous occasions, she would bring together a group of five community and business leaders who wanted to know about Huntsville and its corporate leaders. She would invite speakers to cover a variety of topics, all connected to helping Huntsville recruit different retail and industry. One of the local businessmen would cover the bill.

Bob Ludwig, at that time the new publisher of The Huntsville Times, spoke to the group not long after he moved to Huntsville, but this time Loretta hosted the meeting at her home. Bob had been staying at a hotel, and she thought he might like a home setting instead. The Heritage Club's food was very good, of course; however, the others in the group benefited too from the decision to relocate the meeting. They all enjoyed a delicious menu of fried corn, a beef dish and bananas Foster.

Leaders in Huntsville had long recognized the power of the media in recruiting new industries, corporations and businesses. LeRoy Simms, a former publisher of The Huntsville Times, along with subsequent publisher Bill Green understood that the paper was a huge tool to help or hurt recruitment efforts. The media today still plays a part, although social media has taken much of that exposure and placed it in the hands of individuals. Positive stories always help recruiting efforts.

The takeaway from all the focus groups and conversations with individuals was no surprise: The basics of quality of life are public safety, roads and schools.

A competent and well-equipped Fire Department is a vital component of public safety, and Mayor Spencer invested in the department. Two new fire stations were built during her tenure. The city bought 16 new fire trucks, including two ladder trucks for the taller buildings being constructed around town. When she took office in 1996, the newest fire truck had been purchased in 1983.

Mayor Spencer with $10,000 check to Huntsville Fire & Rescue
from the Fireman's Fund to help with the restoration of the antique fire engine.

While making sure the department had essential upgrades, the mayor also saw the need to preserve some of the department's treasured historical items. Jay Gates, who in 1998 was the department's public information officer, informed her that the department's Ahrens-Fox fire truck, acquired in 1927 for the sum of $12,500, was sitting idle in Station 1, but he believed it had potential. After their discussion – and after Gates showed her, through his mechanical abilities, that the truck could still run – the mayor agreed that it should be saved and restored as close to its former glory as possible.

Mayor Spencer greets the community
during the annual West Huntsville School Parade.

Great detail went into the fire truck's restoration, including the silver alarm bell which had to be rung manually and which required extensive polishing. Bob Wilkerson, who was an owner of Big Spring Bottling, the local Coca-Cola bottler and distributor at that time, took it to Coca-Cola's shop and restored the truck and the bell. Mayor Spencer fully supported its refurbishment by funding the effort in the budget. This effort was also supported by the City Council.

*Mayor Spencer smiles to the crowd while waving an American flag
during a parade in downtown Huntsville. She is riding in
the historic fire truck that was restored with her support.*

Thanks to the determination of Gates – and Mayor Spencer's support
of this historic reminder of days long passed – the 1927 Ahrens-Fox fire
truck became and, as of this writing, still is the lead vehicle in many parades
and is treasured by the community. The mayor made it the lead vehicle
in the annual Christmas Parade, as well as the West Huntsville School
Parade, which began at the Academy for Science and Foreign Language,
passed the Dr. Richard Showers Recreation Center and ended at J.O.
Johnson High School for food, fun and games to begin the school year.

Mayor Spencer's Fire Department focus went beyond the equipment
to the personnel. The city purchased exercise equipment to be placed in all
fire stations within the first three years of her administration. She wanted
firefighters to have a convenient place where they could maintain optimal
physical conditioning to meet physical training testing requirements of
the department.

The mayor combined the police and fire departments in an additional
new station built on Clinton Avenue in 2008.

Also during her administration, a fire station was designed for the southern-most portion of the city, and land was purchased for it as well as for a future police and fire station at Greenbrier. The latter had been a request by Volkswagen when negotiations were active to build a plant in Huntsville. A deal was also made to build a new fire station on Green Mountain.

Improving the Huntsville Police Department and keeping the force well-equipped and staffed was another priority. Working with the police chief and command staff, Mayor Spencer developed three district police precincts, making them more of a neighborhood concept.

Robin Conn/Huntsville Times

Huntsville Mayor Loretta Spencer, left, hugs a lion given to her by DARE officer Lonnie Stone during graduation ceremonies at Holy Spirit recently.

This clipping from The Huntsville Times captures one of Loretta Spencer's many school visits, this time with a DARE officer.

Computers were placed in all police cruisers to aid in efficiency, and duty cars were changed out after 100,000 miles for the safety of the officers. Cars that were taken out of service were used in other departments or were donated to volunteer fire departments in Madison County.

The increase of pedestrian events in Huntsville prompted interest in forming a police bicycle unit. Mayor Spencer recognized the ingenuity of two officers who said they would like to form this unit. She paid for their training at Auburn University during their off-duty time. Then TVA gave the city its first specialized police bike.

Mayor Spencer talks with a Huntsville police officer on duty with the Bike Unit.

The Bike Unit grew and continues to provide safety at public events with officers on bicycles traveling through areas not accessible to police cruisers. You will see them during Concerts in the Park and frequently on weekends in the downtown and Five Points areas. Their presence adds additional safety, making it more enticing for people to frequent downtown restaurants and stroll through the historic districts.

Creating roadways that move traffic safely and efficiently from place to place is a large expense that cities must design, plan and secure. Mayor Spencer's ability to form partnerships paid dividends exponentially with the state highway department.

With a growing population and more jobs coming to Huntsville, the need to expand roadways was pressing in some areas. During her second year in office, Mayor Spencer got the Alabama Department of Transportation (ALDOT), through a retiring ALDOT district engineer, to expand South Memorial Parkway to three lanes from Martin Road to Hobbs Island Road. The increased capacity with the six-lane highway made the road a safer route for the tens of thousands of motorists traveling it daily. The third lanes were added by including an outside lane on each side.

Drivers appreciate expanded roads; however, the traffic jams caused during construction at peak travel times is frustrating and, at times, can produce additional danger. Mayor Spencer addressed this issue by authorizing the city's first night paving project when Airport Road needed to be resurfaced.

Reed Construction worked with the mayor and the necessary city departments to develop the schedule. It was so successful that the same schedule was used during resurfacing on north and south Memorial Parkway and again for the Governors Drive resurfacing over Monte Sano. The company doing the work favored this approach since less traffic on the roadways made the projects safer for workers and travelers alike, and the lower temperatures at night reduced the risk of workers suffering from heat-related health problems.

With road projects as with every other task she tackled, Mayor Spencer focused on details and relationships to make great progress. Noticing that ALDOT bushhogged two times per year and that grass on the

I-565 and Memorial Parkway medians was three-feet tall when she first ran for office, the mayor proposed a partnership. The City of Huntsville would mow the interstates and state right-of-ways, all entryways into the city limits and the median area on the Parkway. ALDOT would pay the city $100,000 annually to help with the cost of purchasing equipment to maintain those areas.

The partnership quickly made a huge difference in the city's overall appearance. Visitors to Huntsville, as well as city residents, could see exactly where the city limits were located. Huntsville was able to maintain an attractive appearance by mowing regularly during peak growing periods. Surrounding cities had grass growth in state rights-of-way that most likely exceeded the limits those cities had placed on residents and businesses to maintain on their properties.

Mayor Spencer took the road cleanup effort one step further by arranging to have litter crews pick up trash before the mowers came through. This policy prevented shredded litter, paper and other trash from topping the freshly mowed grass. These crews were comprised of work-release inmates who volunteered to do the work and have some time outside.

Chapter Sixteen

The Quality of Fun and Games

*G*rowing up in Huntsville, Loretta Spencer was a sports fan as a participant and observer, so she well knew that the fun and games provided by sports facilities are an important part of a city's quality of life – and an attractive tourist draw. That's why she pushed to develop the Huntsville Sports Commission. Not only did it enhance the sports opportunities in Huntsville, this city-created organization brings in lodging and sales tax revenue vital to the city's fiscal strength.

Mayor Spencer knew that many families were traveling great distances to compete in a variety of sports competitions. Her daughter, Sarah, told her how much she was spending – including sometimes having to stay overnight – for her sons' games. So many other families were spending their money in other cities too.

The mayor realized that, with a solid plan and implementation, those dollars plus more could benefit Huntsville. Her plan had two major components. The first was to develop and/or improve the facilities needed to go after large competitions. The second was to establish an entity to seek out the opportunities, bid on them, and, once events were successfully recruited, to organize those events.

Mayor Spencer founded the Huntsville Sports Commission (HSC) in 1999. It was run by a 15-member volunteer board. It hired its first executive director in 2003.

HSC worked closely with city officials to recruit state title events in a variety of sports – from state high school championships in soccer, wrestling, golf and more to the regional Super Retriever Series dog trials. They worked on recruiting girls' volleyball for multiple years. The mayor reached out to local travel soccer organizations to enlist their help in bringing games to Huntsville.

To get Huntsville ready to receive the players and spectators, the city built new sports facilities and improved existing ones.

The Huntsville Women's Tennis Association requested a meeting with Mayor Spencer to discuss potential new facilities, and the mayor agreed to build a complex to host tournaments. Both the mayor and the Tennis Association hoped to lure a tournament from Mobile to the cooler climes of Huntsville. After the construction of the Huntsville Tennis Center, that tournament did move here. The Seniors Tournament followed with people coming from Hawaii and Canada to compete.

Mayor Spencer, right, and a member of the Huntsville Women's Tennis Association. This group encouraged the mayor to build a new tennis complex that would bring tournaments — and their tourist dollars — to town.

Ralph Stone and Mayor Spencer lobbied Alabama High School Athletic Association (AHSAA) Director Dan Washburn to hold the state high school soccer tournament in Huntsville. To entice the AHSAA to move the tournament, the city built the necessary fields and facilities in John Hunt Park. According to an article by John Pruitt in The Huntsville Times on July 1, 2000, the city invested $500,000 for improvements to John Hunt Park to build fields.

Carucha L. Meuse/Huntsville Times

Ralph Stone, the city's director of the Recreation Services and Landscape Management Department, sits in the new stands overlooking one of two fields that will serve as the site for next week's state soccer tournament. Stone, who is a member of the city's Sports Commission, will also direct the 24-team tournament.

Huntsville Sports Commission member Ralph Stone, director of the city's Recreation Services and Landscape Management Department sits in the stands at one of the soccer fields built during Mayor Spencer's administration in this clipping from The Huntsville Times.

Ask anyone who has played on the famous championship fields, and they will tell you the quality of the turf is amazing. Mayor Spencer sent Tony Ivey, who worked in the city's Landscape Management Department, to Auburn University to learn how to maintain the fields so they could drain well after a rain. This was especially important during tournaments. It takes about 30 minutes for the lush fields to drain. During one tournament, rain did delay the start of a game, but the field was so inviting that some of the student-athletes took off their shoes and enjoyed the lush turf with their bare feet.

According to the HSC's website, as of 2011 this entity had held more than 300 sporting events in Huntsville with a total economic impact of more than $108 million for the community.

It is important to emphasize that this revenue was new money, not part of the HSC's regular budget. At year's end, this additional money could be used to replace needed items to keep those sports and visitors coming back to town.

Since the soccer tournament first arrived in Huntsville, David and Rhonda Martin have hosted the media on the day before the tournament begins and during the tournament by grilling, on site, their popular Steak-Out hamburgers and chicken sandwiches. Game officials and state officials are amazed at the hospitality, so the tournament continues to be renewed three years at a time.

With the growing population in Huntsville, it also became apparent that more services and opportunities should be provided for individuals with special needs. Johnnie Franklin, a parent of a special-needs child, met with Mayor Spencer and Steve Ivey, who was the manager of the Recreation Services Department at the time. He asked them to research special playing field surfaces that were available for baseball fields. Recreation Services made trips to other states to do their research. The Civitan Club helped to provide funds for construction. The city formed the Miracle League and built the special-needs ballpark in Brahan Spring Park. Later they named it the Johnnie Franklin Field.

Not long afterwards, the city added sand volleyball courts to Brahan Spring Park after members of the community requested them. HSC researched the possibility of hosting tournaments for the sport in Huntsville.

Huntsville skateboarders

New park opens Saturday for enthusiasts to practice their 360s, 540s on rails and curbs

By KEITH CLINES
Times Staff Writer
kclines@htimes.com

Skateboarders and in-line skaters will finally get a place to call home Saturday

"They won't have to travel to Birmingham or other places to skate where it's legal."

Matt Priest, skateboarder

This clipping from The Huntsville Times announces the opening of the new skateboard park during Mayor Spencer's administration.

Chapter Seventeen

Streamlining City Operations

$\mathcal{A}$ nyone who volunteers with nonprofit organizations knows the importance of managing resources in the most efficient methods to expand operations. When Loretta Spencer became mayor, this veteran volunteer was already an experienced hand at stretching the dollars of any budget. In one of her major initiatives, Mayor Spencer worked with department directors to analyze city operations to make Huntsville's tax dollars work harder. During her three terms, she implemented many changes to reduce expenditures and improve working conditions for employees.

She quickly targeted the City of Huntsville's garbage collection system, which was not automated when she took office. This system was a drain on city coffers as well as a health risk for city employees. Prior to 1996, the city had been subsidizing garbage collection at a rate of $2 million per year. One of the largest costs was due to back injuries suffered by sanitation workers who had to repeatedly lift heavy garbage cans.

Most of the cities around Huntsville – Arab, Athens, Decatur and Scottsboro – were already using automated collection systems. For a city with a reputation for technological innovation, Huntsville was well behind the times in this regard. The mayor realized the city needed to switch to an automated collection system as soon as possible, but this was no small feat. The complete process took four years.

Mayor Spencer held meetings with citizens in all City Council districts to discuss the change. One of the factors would be increasing the garbage fee citizens paid on a monthly basis in order to purchase the necessary trucks for the automated system.

By looking at other cities and considering what might be most appropriate for Huntsville, Mayor Spencer and her team found a way to automate the garbage collection process and have it largely pay its way. Residential garbage was being collected twice weekly. To keep residential costs from increasing, they changed garbage collection to once weekly. This encouraged residents to recycle more so they would have less garbage.

Steve Abbott was the city's public works director when this modification took place.

"I wanted to hire Steve," Mayor Spencer explains, "because he had experience in automating garbage service in Decatur."

Abbott took city employees to Tuscaloosa to see how that city had installed a mechanical arm on the back of existing trucks to pick up trash receptacles until automated trucks could be purchased.

Huntsville phased in the automation process, which quickly became seamless. Households paid an additional $3.50 for weekly household garbage service with a rolling cart provided as well as the weekly removal of yard waste and trash. The monthly price became $14.50.

This change reduced the number of employees needed from three to one per truck. However, there were no reductions in the workforce. Instead, the decrease in employees was handled through attrition. Collection routes were restructured among City Council districts, and the department adopted a four-day work week. Friday would be used as a collection day only during holiday weeks. This made it possible for city employees to enjoy holidays with their families.

"Steve was such an asset to the department and the city because he had so much experience," Mayor Spencer said of Abbott. "The department became fiscally sound with his leadership."

Collecting garbage is a messy business. The unsightliness of the sanitation trucks ran counter to Mayor Spencer's vision for an attractive, welcoming city. For residents and visitors alike, she wanted the trucks driving through city neighborhoods to be as clean as possible. To keep the mess to a minimum, Huntsville constructed a truck washing facility and established a schedule for washing the trucks regularly. Kathy Hunt, who was the Sanitation Department manager, was instrumental in this process.

The Public Works Department, much like Public Safety, can be called into action for many reasons and at any time. When Mayor Spencer was considering hiring Abbott, he asked her if his living in Decatur would be a problem. Her response: "Not so long as you can be here when the first snowflake falls."

In previous years when there was snow and ice, the snow clearing process would leave ice behind. The mayor wanted to change that. The Public Works Department would take a proactive approach when bad weather was predicted. Salt and barricades would be deployed in advance, ready for speedier placement for enhanced safety.

Mayor Spencer continued to lead with progressive thinking and brainstorming among departments to develop best practices.

Landscape Management began keeping equipment within the district they were servicing. These centralized locations eliminated the inefficient use of time and fuel to drive equipment back and forth.

When looking at the money spent to repair large city vehicles, it became clear that an internal repair shop would be fiscally beneficial. In 2008 Mayor Spencer set aside $1 million from a TIF to build a repair shop facility for the city instead of contracting the work. This facility was built in 2009 after her last term. While the brick-and-mortar site did not get completed while she was in office, she is pleased to see that this visionary move still serves the city well at the time of this writing.

Better bond ratings

Maximizing tax dollars and streamlining services had other rewards with additional benefits that paid dividends the city still reaps: better bond ratings.

When Mayor Spencer took office in 1996, the city was in debt, and its bond rating was only an A.

"An early goal was to pay down the debt and go after a AA bond rating," she said.

Mayor Spencer's fiscal year 1998 budget was projected to be in the black, according to an editorial board report in The Huntsville Times on Oct. 20, 1997. The bond rating agency Standard & Poor's issued that AA bond rating for the City of Huntsville in 1998. In the Nov. 5, 1998, edition of The Huntsville Times, Phil Dotts noted, "Only 2 percent of cities are awarded this rating."

The bond market obviously liked what the City of Huntsville was doing under Mayor Spencer's leadership. In just two years, Huntsville went from being in debt with a pattern of increasing debt to carrying over money and paying down debt. The last two years of Mayor Spencer's administration saw a carry-over of $15 million each year.

This tight fiscal management continued to pay off beyond her administration. In January 2009, three months after she left office, the City of Huntsville earned a AAA rating, the highest level.

Mayor Spencer gives a great deal of credit for the city's steadily improving financial outlook to city Finance Director Randy Taylor. She had searched long and hard for a highly qualified person to appoint for this job. She remembered that he had performed audits in the past for the city.

"I hired Randy in February 1998, but I had to wait until June 1 for him to come to the city because the company he was working for had a year-end in May," she said. "He was definitely worth waiting for."

Mayor Spencer said it was important for her and Taylor to have the same goals. She had inherited a city in debt, and she needed to pay down that debt and take care of city employees to ensure the city's healthy growth.

They spent hours setting goals to stay on track with city salaries because 73 percent of the annual budget paid the cost of operation.

The growth plan included new retail businesses that would bring in new taxes that would to go to Huntsville City Schools' operations. Funds brought in by economic development progress would resurface roads and fill the needs expressed by city department directors. Big ticket items were consistently requested by department directors to operate their departments.

"We continued to keep our eyes on the bottom line while looking for ways to take care of employees and improve department operations," Mayor Spencer said.

Sometimes, improving department operations involved making sure that the right people were in the right position. The mayor hired Mia Puckett to be the city's Equal Employment Opportunity Commission officer. She knew Mia from Junior League. Mia's law background was a definite asset to the position. Then, when the director of the Human Resources Department left for another opportunity, the mayor already had the next department leader close at hand. The mayor appointed Mia as department director, a position Mia held through the end of the Spencer administration.

When looking at the city's Animal Services Department, Mayor Spencer quickly saw that the department would benefit from having a veterinarian as the director. She appointed Dr. Lisa Jackson as the first veterinarian to be director of the department. Dr. Jackson had worked with the federal government and had vast experience with many different types of animals. She remained in the position until leaving to buy an existing private practice in Huntsville.

The benefits of having a veterinarian's experience leading the Animal Services Department established a precedent that continued when the next director, Dr. Karen Hill Sheppard, was hired in 2002. She retired from the position in early 2024.

As a former teacher, Mayor Spencer always looked for ways to improve programs involving youth. When it was time to appoint a municipal judge, she chose someone whom she knew shared those concerns. The Honorable Judge Lynn Sherrod did a wonderful job working with youth on appropriate alternative sentencing. Sherrod was appointed as a district judge in Madison County's 23rd District in 1999 and went on to become the first African American to win an at-large election in North Alabama, according to an article in the Oct. 12, 2012, issue of The Huntsville Times.

At Judge Sherrod's retirement, her comments to Mayor Spencer were very meaningful. She thanked Spencer for the opportunity given to her in 1997 with that appointment. For the mayor, the appointment was easy: Sherrod was the right person for that position.

During Mayor Spencer's last term, she rehired Richard Kramer in the Traffic Engineering Department. He had retired, but he was a true expert in analyzing and improving traffic operations. He brought a renewed level of detail to the way Huntsville approached providing the means for traffic to move efficiently and safely around the city. He and Jahazy Rooks, whom Spencer also appointed during her last term as the director of Information

Technology Services, collaborated to bring many new tools to Huntsville commuters.

One project was the installation of several traffic cameras in 2007 to give people a view of driving conditions on major thoroughfares. In 2008, the city was ready to implement a traffic information system that would have put information regarding traffic flow and volume across the city easily accessible on the internet. That information is now readily available on smart phones.

Kramer often teased Mayor Spencer about her many ideas concerning the city's traffic situation. She spent a lot of time driving to meetings and events across the city, so her usual response to him was, "I have a lot of experience with traffic in Huntsville."

Chapter Eighteen

Redstone Arsenal
and Military Relationships

Redstone Arsenal had just under 700 active duty soldiers and more than 50,000 civilian and contract employees in 2023, according to Military Installations, an official Defense Department website. That makes it the largest employer by far in the Huntsville-Madison County metropolitan area.

It's hard to imagine that such a powerful economic engine as the Arsenal was almost shut down way back when Loretta Spencer was a child growing up in Huntsville. The Office of the Assistant Secretary of the Army directed that the post be advertised for sale by July 1, 1949. The Corps of Engineers placed a sign, shown at top left, at the Arsenal entrance. What had started as a controversial project was set to be dismissed altogether.

Fortunately for Huntsville, that didn't happen. NASA and the team of German rocket scientists arrived, and Redstone Arsenal expanded instead. According to the U.S. Department of Housing and Urban Development (March 19, 2018), Redstone Arsenal has an annual economic impact of at least $10.8 million on North Alabama.

Loretta Spencer was well aware of the value of the relationship between Redstone Arsenal and the City of Huntsville when she became mayor in 1996. Her strong professional and personal relationships with the people whose military careers brought them to Huntsville could fill its own book. As a volunteer, as the mayor and as a resident, she has consistently shown how much she holds the military and their families in high esteem.

The mayor's first major demonstration of that support involved a huge boost in Redstone's personnel.

Bringing home BRAC

The U.S. Department of Defense's Base Realignment and Closure (BRAC) process closed more than 350 military bases and shifted many military operations from one base to another starting with the 1988 round. Redstone Arsenal benefitted from two BRAC moves in 1995 and 2005. They increased the number of government defense entities in Huntsville as well as the presence of contractors to support the mission of Team Redstone.

During the implementation of Redstone's first BRAC in 1995, the Aviation Command relocated from St. Louis, Missouri, to Huntsville. To help make the move as smooth as possible for the community's new residents, Mayor Spencer coordinated the One-Stop, a combined city, county and state effort set up in the former Parkway City Mall. This happened during the time when half of the mall was vacant. The One-Stop opened at the end of June 1997 and remained open until Oct. 1, 1997.

The One-Stop made it possible for new residents to get everything needed in one location to set up residence, including driver license, vehicle license plate, animal license, utility service, school registration and telephone service. They also could find information on recreational sports for children and health department records. It was open Monday through Friday from 9 a.m. to 5 p.m.

Two City Council assistants manned the One-Stop for the city daily by rotating shifts. Many of the people relocating did not know where they would move, so all three municipalities – Huntsville, Madison and Madison County – were represented.

Word spread quickly that Huntsville was a great place to live. People who had transferred would relay back to friends, relatives and former co-workers that they did not regret their decision to move.

Many of the people relocating here were surprised to board a bus touring the area and find that Mayor Spencer was taking the time to ride with them and tell them about Huntsville. They, like the people she met on the recruiting trips, left with her direct phone number. She would personally take their calls. Needless to say, many of the calls were requests from people with a variety of special circumstances.

From time to time, Loretta Spencer still encounters people who mention the One-Stop and her welcoming bus rides because they made such a positive impression. Unfortunately for the 2005 BRAC, the One-Stop wasn't possible because the moves were made during a three-year period, much longer than during Huntsville's first BRAC.

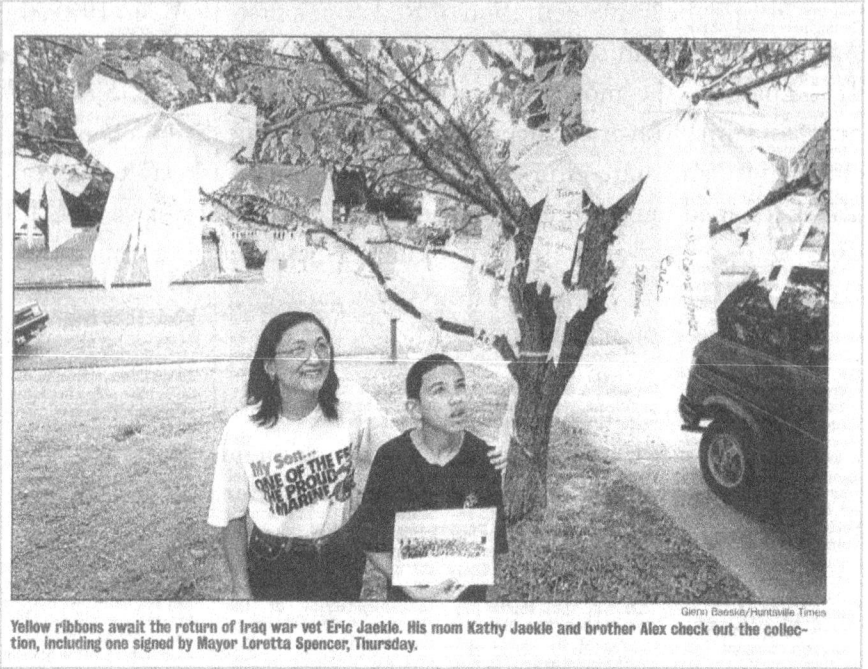

Yellow ribbons await the return of Iraq war vet Eric Jaekle. His mom Kathy Jaekle and brother Alex check out the collection, including one signed by Mayor Loretta Spencer, Thursday.

One of the many ways Mayor Spencer showed her unwavering support
for deployed troops and their families was signing a yellow ribbon
decorating the yard of Iraq war vet Eric Jaekle.

Housing the generals

Long after the 1995 transfers were complete, BRAC remained a top priority of Mayor Spencer. To help Redstone Arsenal compete for the 2005 BRAC move, she targeted better housing as key to success. Most generals chose to live off post due to the Arsenal's outdated and substandard housing. One officer's wife said, "It was like side-by-side trailers." The mayor was determined to change that.

When Mayor Spencer took office in 1996, there were only one-star generals living at Redstone. The 2005 BRAC would mean that two- and three-star generals would be living on post, as well as a four-star.

The team sent word to the Pentagon, making a "no strings attached" offer that the city would build houses for generals on Redstone land. The

Pentagon sent back the specifications for the generals' houses that the city would have to meet, but there was doubt within the Pentagon that the city would fulfill the promise.

Redstone's garrison commander, Col. Robert Devlin, provided updates on amenities and requirements. This was a huge help during the two years that went into planning the houses for the generals.

At that time, the existing houses for generals dated back to Mayor Spencer's childhood in Huntsville. Some were from the 1940s and some from the 1950s. They were substandard and in definite need of replacement. The mayor recalls visiting friends who lived in those houses when she was in elementary school. Children living on the Arsenal were assigned to Fifth Avenue Elementary School, where she attended.

The summer before she first ran for office, she sat at a Huntsville Stars baseball game with Lieutenant General Jim Link and his wife, Judy, who told her about the problems with the living conditions on post.

With memories from her childhood combined with the descriptions from these newer friends, Mayor Spencer knew that building better houses for Redstone's generals was essential for the Arsenal and Huntsville to win the 2005 BRAC round. She established a three-person building authority to pay attention to the financing of the houses. She chose Bob Ludwig, publisher of The Huntsville Times, because she knew he would make sure that everything was done correctly.

"Bob kept the ship a sail," she recalls.

Past projects with the other two members made her confident in their abilities to keep everything progressing appropriately.

Mayor Spencer knew the city needed to build 10 new houses. To fund the project, she would have to make a deal with the governor, so she did.

She negotiated first with Gov. Don Siegelman to pay for roadways. In their discussions, he suggested swapping the money which she knew was in the budget for roadways and major roadwork. With the state bearing the costs for roadwork, this left City of Huntsville funds to be used to pay for the first three houses.

The mayor made the same agreement with Siegelman's successor, Gov. Bob Riley, when seven more houses were needed. Riley quickly saw that the project was beneficial not only to Huntsville and to the whole state of Alabama.

Ludwig, who was chairman of the Federal Building Authority, helped to finalize the agreements.

When the agreement had to go before the City Council for approval, two council members voted against it. It still passed with three votes. However, Mayor Spencer had hoped the vote would be unanimous since news would travel back to Washington, D.C. Unfortunately the 3-to-2 vote temporarily caused the military to doubt that the community would be supportive. It was especially surprising because one "no" vote came from a member with strong ties to the military.

The vote turned out to be a minor setback that was overcome eventually. The benefits of the project continue to be felt. Building the generals' quarters strengthened the reputation of Huntsville and Mayor Spencer as partners who valued the military and were willing to invest in amenities that would be appreciated by them. During one of the mayor's visits to the Pentagon, a lieutenant general she knew from his business visits to Huntsville remarked, "Oh, you are the mayor building the generals' houses."

Along with meeting the Pentagon specifications for the houses, everyone working on the project wanted them to have a sense of style that would fit into the larger Huntsville community. Peter Lowe looked through Southern Living house plans to find just the right one that would satisfy Pentagon requirements. The idea was to find a basic plan and adjust the exterior features and some interior features.

Mayor Spencer chose several trusted residents to review the plan that had been selected. Betsy Lowe, Jeanne McCown and Jane Walker Troup held a Southern ladies' lunch to look at the chosen plan. Judy Link happened to be in town and asked to join them. Timing could not have been more perfect. She had been living in generals' quarters with her husband and family, so her input was invaluable.

When they opened the carefully chosen plan, Judy quickly told them they could not build that house. The ladies were a bit surprised. They wondered if they had they overlooked some regulation.

No, there was nothing wrong with the house. Coincidentally, Judy was building that exact house in Huntsville. Everyone agreed it was a beautiful house, but they picked another beautiful plan instead.

Lieutenant General James "Jim" Pillsbury and his wife, Becky, were the first family to move into one of the houses at 1 Cribbens Court. Several generals stationed at Redstone Arsenal who were anticipating living in the houses were given other assignments instead.

Lieutenant General Larry Dodgen, who had two commands in Huntsville, and his wife just missed out on one of the new houses. They lived next door to the house that was being built, and he liked to joke that he saw every brick being laid. That house was finished just a few weeks before Dodgen had to return to D.C., and Brigadier General Samuel Cannon and his wife became its first occupants instead.

To commemorate the completion of that house before he left Huntsville, Dodgen and his wife and the Pillsburys shared pizza on the dining room floor of the Pillsburys' new home. Their furniture had not yet arrived.

When the finished houses were previewed, many military visitors were surprised that the walls weren't totally white. White was required in most military housing. The colors of the walls drew such interest that one wife of a visiting general who came from Fort Campbell for the Change of Command ceremony wanted to know which paint colors had been approved so she could use those in their house. Mayor Spencer had this information at hand and quickly gave her a paint sample.

Mayor Spencer invested her time to get to know generals and their spouses who are stationed in Huntsville. Each year she hosted a Holiday Brunch at her home with special gifts for them, and she continued this tradition for many years after she left office. She understands that relationships should be built genuinely, not just opportunistically.

"During my first administration, the military took me under their wing," she said. "They were not going to let me fail."

She realized the importance of the strength of this relationship between City of Huntsville officials and Redstone Arsenal. It is hard to fully state how unusual it was for a city to make this much of an investment. Needless to say, it has paid off.

Space & Missile Defense Symposium

Mayor Spencer credits some of her early acquaintances with the military to Brigadier General (retired) Dan Montgomery and his wife, Phyllis. He encouraged the mayor to attend a conference in El Paso, Texas. She went, and it was the first time a mayor from Huntsville had gone to the Space & Missile Defense Symposium.

The mayor didn't miss a single booth. She was informed that her attendance was a popular topic at the conference. Her female military escort said everyone kept remarking, "She got here. She's coming to our conference."

Mayor Spencer was able to meet with VIPs of major companies. Most of these VIPs were not coming to Huntsville on regular business at that time. Many of them had corporate offices in Texas and California – a good distance from Alabama. Being able to talk with them in person gave her the opportunity to sell them on Huntsville.

She also met many military officers who would eventually come to Huntsville. That's where she first got to know General John "Jack" Costello and his wife, Micki. He was a conference speaker, and the mayor had lunch with him, Micki and the mayor of El Paso.

During this visit, Mayor Spencer was asked if Huntsville could host the mid-year conference for Space & Missile Defense. "Yes" was her immediate answer. Of course, the man who asked was not aware of her experience on the VBC board and that she formed the Convention & Visitors Bureau, housed at that time in the VBC. She recognized this was an opportunity for Huntsville to earn the reputation for doing things the right way on a large stage.

That afternoon they announced that next year the conference would be held in Huntsville, Alabama. Spencer clapped from the audience. She was the only one clapping in the audience of 300. This was a multiple-year contract for a high profile meeting with representatives from many countries.

Coincidentally, Col. Troy Trulock was also the mayor's military escort on that first visit. Trulock would later be elected mayor of Madison, Huntsville's neighboring city.

Mayor Spencer knew that Huntsville's representation at conferences would put the city in contention to host some of the large defense conferences. This would extend to selling corporations on Huntsville. The result would be an impressive economic impact directly from hosting these conferences – as well as the expansion of companies to Huntsville which would bring more jobs to the region.

With the community's support, this plan worked. Large conferences now see Huntsville as an attractive conference/convention location. The Space & Missile Defense Symposium has been held annually in Huntsville since 1997. It is considered the premier conference for the U.S. and its allies from around the world.

Montgomery continued to involve Mayor Spencer in military matters. He nominated her for the Honorable Order of Saint Barbara during her first term as mayor. She considers this one of her most notable military honors.

Mayor Spencer understood military protocol, but she also remembered the importance of personal details. Ginger Stephens, who worked in the AMCOM Congressional Affairs office for 24 years, was a huge help when the mayor sent small remembrances to her military friends – including boxes of Krispy Kreme doughnuts.

9/11 and afterward

The strength of the bond that Mayor Spencer forged with local military commanders made a united presence during the terrorist attacks on Sept. 11, 2001. Lieutenant General Larry Dodgen had been sworn in as Redstone's commanding general the day before. As the nation learned the extent of the attacks on U.S. soil, the mayor and the general were in constant contact. No one knew how many locations would be targeted or where they might be. During one of the many conversations they had that day, the mayor remembers the general asking her, "May I call you Loretta?"

The friendship between Loretta and the Dodgen family began then and lasted during her time in office and afterwards. The mayor even became friends with the general's mother after meeting her at the swearing-in

Photo by Connie Davis

Special induction... '99

Huntsville Mayor Loretta Spencer is inducted into the Order of Saint Barbara and awarded a Saint Barbara medal by Brig. Gen. Dan Montgomery, program executive officer for air and missile defense. This took place Nov. 13 during the Redstone Arsenal/Huntsville Chapter, Air Defense Artillery Association luncheon at the Redstone Arsenal Club.

The Order of Saint Barbara is one of Loretta Spencer's most cherished honors.

ceremony, and they also stayed in contact. Each year at Mardi Gras time, the elder Mrs. Dodgen, who lived in New Orleans, would send a King Cake to the mayor's office for the staff to enjoy. She would call to be sure the cake was received in good order. The mayor remembers that Mrs. Dodgen always wanted to know who found the small plastic baby in the cake.

"It was very evident that Huntsville became extended family for those who relocated here," Mayor Spencer said.

Military service members and their families have always held a special place in Mayor Spencer's heart. They remained a focus throughout her administration, especially in the wake of the 9/11 terrorist attacks and the military response by the U.S.

"The battles on foreign soil became so close to me with so many residents and employees being deployed," she recalls.

To show appreciation and support for the deployed soldiers and their families, she never missed a deployment ceremony or a return. She also made sure the returning soldiers had a police escort.

She recalls one particular visit with a soldier that gave her a deeper understanding of the trials and sacrifices soldiers experience during deployment. Not only were their lives and safety at stake, he told her, but they also faced the everyday irritants of sand-saturating food, clothing, hair and basically everything. Along with all they had to overcome, they missed their families and friends back home.

The community came together in 2001 in so many ways, and Mayor Spencer did what she could to encourage this unity. One simple way was to have bumper stickers printed with "We Stand United" and the image of the America flag and to distribute them at central locations. The goal was to have them on every vehicle as a constant reminder of support for those deployed and their families. This was one of those smaller details that Mayor Spencer knew could make a big impact.

Mayor Spencer welcomed Redstone generals and their families as new neighbors in her growing city that hadn't lost its small-town feel – and she even included weather alerts in her welcome. During one tornado warning, she personally called Marilyn Phillips, who had moved here recently with her husband, Lieutenant General Bill Phillips. She wanted to make sure that they were aware of the danger and ready to take the proper precautions. The Phillipses were the only ones in that area that day. The other families living on Cribbens Court were out of town. Fortunately, the tornado skipped over the Arsenal.

Marilyn and Bill Phillips are one of the many military families who have chosen to settle in the Huntsville area after serving on the Arsenal and becoming involved in the community. After retiring, the general returned to Huntsville as the vice president of Army programs at The Boeing Company.

Redstone Arsenal is not just an entity. It's also the life's work of so many people, both enlisted and civilian. People give their talents and dedicate their careers to bettering and protecting the nation.

"I had a genuine interest in what was happening at Redstone with an appreciation of the milestones and successes there," Mayor Spencer said. "The real-life events that transpired were important."

As part of the city's efforts to support American troops deployed during the wars in Iraq and Afghanistan, Mayor Spencer had yellow ribbons tied around trees in Big Spring International Park. Across the country, displaying yellow ribbons was a popular way of showing support for the troops.

Mutual support

The strong relationship between Mayor Spencer and the commanders of Redstone Arsenal was mutual. During her first two weeks in office, Lieutenant General Jim Link, took the mayor on a fly-over of Redstone in a helicopter. To her surprise, they flew with the doors open.

"People asked me if I was a bit afraid during the flight. Honestly, I was more concerned about my purse falling out of the helicopter than any safety issues."

She had placed her purse between her feet on the floor. Later she found out that there was an option to have the doors closed.

"I didn't know I had a choice," she replied when asked if she'd flown with the doors open or closed.

While in flight, they also took a path over Cummings Research Park, which gave the mayor a new perspective of the success of this project which placed Fortune 500 companies in the former agricultural fields. She had worked on that project from day one and wanted to see it from the sky.

Mayor Spencer holds special memories of all the various Redstone commanders.

Major General John Holley made sure that she was informed about the work Redstone Arsenal touched. He would call her from missile test sites to let her know when there had been a successful test of ground-based missile interceptors.

When talks were initiated between the U.S. and Poland for placement of interceptor missiles there, Mayor Spencer was in touch with senior-level Polish officials. The similarities between Huntsville and Slupsk, Poland, at that time made the conversation easy. Huntsville's international community also made finding a Polish interpreter, in less than two days, a small hurdle to overcome for a meeting via Skype between the two leaders. The meeting achieved its goal and also resulted in an unexpected invitation for a delegation from Huntsville to attend a significant celebration in Slupsk as guests of the state.

Whenever she was asked what advice she would give regarding developing relationships with the military as well as businesses, Mayor Spencer

Carucha L. Meuse/Huntsville Times

Huntsville Mayor Loretta Spencer shakes the hands of the men and women of Bravo Company during a deployment ceremony Friday in Guntersville.

It was a priority of Mayor Spencer to attend deployment ceremonies during the wars in Iraq and Afghanistan to express her appreciation to the troops.

stressed what she learned early on during her years as a volunteer: Extend hospitality and listen well.

Each year during Armed Forces Week, she held a special catered picnic for the generals and their wives who were based here during the Monday night Concerts in the Park. That concert always featured a military band brought in for the event. She also made sure to invite the wives to events in the community that would be of interest to them. She wanted them to feel like Huntsville was their home instead of just one more stop during the many moves made during military careers.

Military officers and their family members have responded in kind with many remaining active in various community organizations after their time in the armed forces ends. One example is the Wreaths for Veterans program. Military wives Phyllis Montgomery and Joy Parker chair this program at all cemeteries in Huntsville and Madison. Each year around

6,000 wreaths are placed on graves to honor those who served. It is a huge undertaking and shows how much the military means to Huntsville in more than one way.

Military families, like all families, experience life trials. In Huntsville they found a caring community to support them through those ups and downs.

14 December 2003

Dear Loretta,

Teri and I so enjoyed brunch yesterday. The meal was simply delicious and it was a wonderful opportunity to meet with many of our community leaders. It is always heart-warming to experience the support our military receives from such a wonderful community.

Merry Christmas,
John

Thank you note from Major General John Holley. Mayor Spencer enjoyed making the generals feel welcome to Huntsville.

4 November 2003

Dear Loretta,

Thank you so much for the West Point coin. It is just beautiful and it will mean a lot to me forever.

It was good to see you during my short visit to Huntsville. Of course, it's always great for me to get "home" to Alabama.

Thank you for all you do for our service men and women.

Sincerely,
Jon Caldwell

Thank you note from Lieutenant General John Caldwell. Mayor Spencer appreciated the military and its important role in the Huntsville community, and she made sure the service men and women and their families felt right at home.

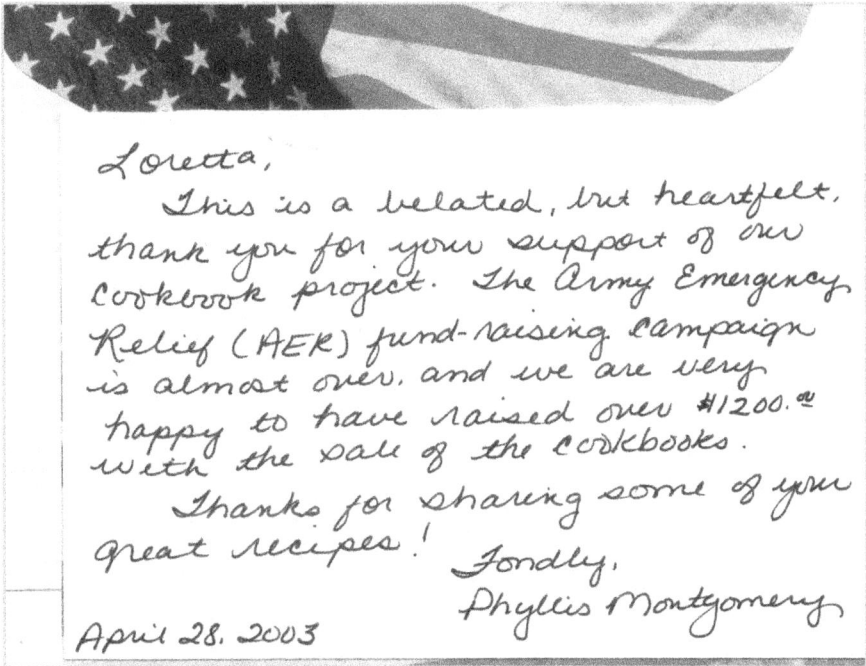

Loretta,

This is a belated, but heartfelt, thank you for your support of our cookbook project. The Army Emergency Relief (AER) fund-raising campaign is almost over, and we are very happy to have raised over $1200.⁰⁰ with the sale of the cookbooks.

Thanks for sharing some of your great recipes!

Fondly,
Phyllis Montgomery

April 28, 2003

Mayor Spencer's support for the military was unwavering – and even extended to sharing some of her recipes with a cookbook fundraising project for Army Emergency Relief.

Chapter Nineteen

Huntsville Hospitality

*H*untsville is known as a welcoming city. That was Huntsville's reputation when Loretta Spencer and her family moved to town in the 1940s, and that remained the city's reputation as it grew significantly throughout Mayor Spencer's tenure. Many generations of city leaders, the mayor among them, made sure that Huntsville's growth never came at the price of losing its spirit of hospitality, so valued in neighborly small Southern towns.

Hurricane Katrina

Mayor Spencer's experience served the whole community well after Hurricane Katrina devastated the Gulf Coast and Huntsville opened its arms to the people who had lost so much in that tragedy.

During that time, Huntsville was also dealing with a tragedy at home – the loss of a young police officer, Daniel Golden, who was killed in the line of duty. After returning from his funeral, Mayor Spencer held an important meeting to address the needs of families relocating to Huntsville with LaFreeda Jordan from U.S. Sen. Richard Shelby's office, Lisa Montgomery from U.S. Sen. Jeff Sessions' office and a staff member from U.S. Rep. Bud Cramer's office as well as the director of the local American Red Cross and a representative from Huntsville City Schools.

The city departments and community pulled together resources in a very short time to make it as easy as possible for people coming here to continue with everyday life, especially the children making the transition to new schools.

Ten doctors volunteered to take at least 10 new patients/families without insurance cards until those could be replaced. Mayor Spencer thanks Dr. Tim Howard for helping to make that happen.

The city set up a one-stop shop, much like the one organized for the families who moved from St. Louis to Huntsville for the first BRAC. Here, the families fleeing the Katrina devastation could replace or request replacement of valuable documents, and parents could enroll their children in school.

Unexpected resources helped supply basic needs. A pro basketball team had recently played at the Von Braun Center and left unopened crates of unused deodorant. Those items, along with food from the Food Bank, beverages from the Coca-Cola Company and other necessities, were gathered in grocery bags for people to take with them to their temporary residences. Many were staying with family members or in the homes of business friends. These items may seem small, but for people who had lost so much and had their lives thoroughly disrupted, these welcoming gifts were invaluable.

The children of Mayor Spencer's son, J, attended Weatherly Heights Elementary. The school opened spare space in the library for people to bring clothing to make it convenient for those in need to get items quickly.

Community businesses renovated a former hotel that had been closed. With the help of local churches, it became the home for more than 500 people during this time. It remained available for six months. Mayor Spencer made time to volunteer with the clean-up effort because Huntsville's newest residents needed to be housed quickly.

Mayor Spencer always stresses that these large community aid programs were team efforts. On many occasions Sharon King, who worked in the mayor's office, and Joy McKee, the coordinator for Operation Green Team at the time, were helping to organize these efforts with others from City Hall. City employees would say, "Count me in too!" and would join so many efforts to help others in the city and surrounding communities.

HUD and the World Changers

Hospitality extends also to those living close to you. This was seen in programs that the city secured or welcomed to the community. Jerry Galloway, longtime director of the city's Community Development Department, had experience working with the U.S. Department of Housing and Urban Development (HUD). During his tenure, the department made huge strides in improving economically challenged areas of the city.

Each July until Jerry's retirement, the World Changers volunteer organization would bring 300 or more youth volunteers and adults to work in neighborhoods. The city would furnish supplies through HUD funding.

The department also secured funding for the Emergency Home Repair program. Each year around 38 homes would be chosen from program applicants for exterior improvements such as new roofs, painting, siding or wheelchair ramps. The Community Development Department would purchase the supplies needed. Volunteers came from all walks of life. Fraternities, churches and businesses were often spending Saturdays working to help those in the community. On more than one occasion, the resident was so thankful to receive the assistance that they insisted on providing a meal for the volunteers. And also on more than one occasion, the volunteers found that the resident was food insecure with little to eat, and the volunteers provided groceries to help the individual or family.

Throughout her time as a volunteer, a civic leader and on into elected office, Mayor Spencer was known for her attention to detail and her natural affinity for quickly identifying efficient action plans, whatever the situation. After she left office, businesses, organizations and entities continued to seek her guidance and involvement to achieve milestones and goals.

"When you have been an active volunteer, serving on many boards before becoming mayor, it is easy to be aware of whom to seek out help from," she said. "You learn how to see the picture fully if you've had experience in your community. Experience is a great asset."

Loretta,

Thanks so much for the delicious candies you sent for my birthday.

You are so nice to have remembered! Bob R. G

Bob Riley
Governor

Thank you note from then-Gov. Bob Riley for the candy Mayor Spencer sent him on his birthday. She enjoyed sending small treats and remembrances to friends she worked with in government, the military and industry.

JEFF SESSIONS
ALABAMA

UNITED STATES SENATE
WASHINGTON, D. C. 20510-0104

December 29, 2003

The Honorable Loretta Spencer
Mayor
City of Huntsville
Post Office Box 308
Huntsville, Alabama 35804-0308

Dear Loretta:

Thank you for the delicious Christmas goodies which were enjoyed by all of my family. You are very kind to think of us at this special time of year.

I look forward to working with you and all the great folks in Huntsville in the upcoming year. Best wishes for a Happy New Year!

Very truly yours,

Jeff Sessions
United States Senator

JS:ph

Thank you note from U.S. Sen. Jeff Sessions. Sharing Christmas goodies was one way Mayor Spencer showed her appreciation to the people who helped her make Huntsville an even better place to live.

Chapter Twenty

The Importance
of the Personal Touch

*M*ost of the work that went on behind the doors of City Hall was serious business for Huntsville and its residents. Whether acting behind or beyond those doors, Mayor Spencer also addressed a wide range of circumstances and concerns of her constituents, including city employees, with her characteristic personal touch. Sometimes she would be congratulating people on joyful occasions or encouraging others during stressful situations. Several times she was on hand to offer sympathy during moments of deep sorrow.

Mayor Spencer said she will never forget the tragedy of Nov. 20, 2006, when a Huntsville City Schools bus carrying students from Lee High School went over the side of an elevated portion of Interstate 565 near downtown and plunged almost 40 feet. Four students, Christine Collier, Nicole Ford, Tanesha Hill and Crystal Renee McCrary, died. Thirty-three others were injured.

The crash happened right next to the city's Public Transportation & Parking facility, and Tommy Brown, the department director, immediately called the mayor and arranged for her to be transported quickly to the site.

"There were injured children everywhere," Mayor Spencer remembers. "They were all upset and hurt, but they were trying to help each other out. I stayed about 20 to 30 minutes and then they took me to the hospital, to the Emergency Room. The students were brought there first."

Glenn Baeske/Huntsville Times

Four Christmas sculptures in Wellman Family Park at Five Points honor the four Lee High students killed in November.

Mayor Spencer will never forget the Lee High School bus crash that killed four students on Nov. 20, 2006, and she made sure their memories would be honored with this Christmas display in Five Points each year.

She helped break the devastating news to the families of the four students.

"The CEO of Huntsville Hospital was new to the area," she said, "and he asked me to go with him to talk to the families."

Leading Huntsville in mourning the loss of those bright, young students – as well as the deaths in the line of duty of Huntsville Police Officer Daniel Howard Golden on Aug. 29, 2005, and Officer William Eric Freeman on Dec. 15, 2007 – was a difficult duty, but the mayor felt this was essential.

Special ways to say 'thank you'

Mayor Spencer always appreciated the hard work of city employees, and she wanted them to know that their efforts were being noticed – especially when bad weather threatened. Employees in many departments would be surprised to arrive at work early in the morning to find the mayor dropping off food for them on a cold winter day. The mayor thought this personal "thank you" was especially important when employees might have to work through the night to keep the roads safe and clear.

Each year around Thanksgiving, Mayor Spencer and Kathy Hunt, manager of the Sanitation Department, would deliver bags of fresh Krispy Kreme doughnuts and water to employees on their routes. At that time of the year, these crews were completing a rigorous effort to vacuum all leaves across the city so curbs would be clean for the many holiday gatherings.

The refreshments were a welcome surprise, but the significance of the mayor and their boss taking time to deliver these treats to each person while they were working made a lasting impression.

"These individuals were working so hard to make the cleanup happen for residents," Mayor Spencer said when asked why this effort was so important to her. "The least we could do was pick up a little treat for them."

These expressions of appreciation did not come from City of Huntsville coffers. Mayor Spencer personally paid for them and many other things.

Police officers would often find their food had been paid for by Mayor Spencer when she went through a fast-food drive-thru ahead of them. This is something she has continued to do since leaving public office. She was paying it forward before it became a popular thing to do, and it is a nice gesture she still enjoys doing.

There were many times that she would remember the city's custodial employees with a special treat too. She appreciated these hard workers who would go the extra mile to make sure offices and surrounding areas looked clean and professional.

Riding with HEMSI

Early in her administration, Mayor Spencer would ride with HEMSI on Friday nights from 4:30 until after 10 p.m. – sometimes even later.

"It was a lesson to see how our emergency services interact between police, fire, HEMSI and the Rescue Squad," she said.

She also wanted to see the variety and severity of some of the calls they had to handle. Experiences on these ride-alongs showed that there was a strong need for a hospital in Madison long before that facility became a reality.

Along with leading the city's transportation department, Tommy Brown was also a member of HEMSI's board of directors. He and Don Webster along with Jon Howell, the HEMSI director, would meet and kept the mayor aware of the details of what they were seeing in the community. But the mayor witnessed all this firsthand many times. She rode along with HEMSI so often that they presented her with her own HEMSI jacket and name badge.

Keeping an open office

During Mayor Spencer's first term, she began a Holiday Open House for all employees. They were invited to come to the eighth floor where the mayor's office was located and enjoy a large variety of holiday goodies made by the mayor herself. They could also meet employees from different departments whose paths they might cross on future projects. This helped to unify departments by building relationships and proved beneficial when departments needed to work together.

In addition to remarks about the delicious food, most employees said they had never been invited to the mayor's office before. They also had never experienced such an investment of the mayor's personal time and money to prepare food to feed 500 or more employees in appreciation for their work. The open house also gave the mayor the chance to personally wish them a happy holiday.

Mayor Spencer had an open-door policy for employees and made them feel welcome whenever they came to the eighth floor. She made sure to include hospitable details, like hot cider available from Thanksgiving through New Year's Eve for the enjoyment of everyone – from representatives of companies that might move to town to visiting dignitaries to the many people responsible for making Huntsville work every day. She recognized the employees as one of the city's greatest assets.

Even today, the mayor runs into city employees who fondly recall their days of working together. While she was compiling this book, such an encounter reminded her about an instance early in her administration when a couple of employees asked her if they could paint the rocket on display at the southwest corner of Airport Road and Memorial Parkway. They told her that it was in bad shape with peeling paint. They offered to buy the paint themselves and do the work on their own time. Grateful for their initiative and pride in their city, she said, "Yes!"

These men felt comfortable bringing this request directly to Mayor Spencer because, during her first few months in office, she made herself accessible to employees so they could get to know her.

An example of this type of outreach was the home-cooked breakfasts that the mayor and her assistant, Janice Fowler, would deliver to all 17 fire stations as early as 5 a.m. Then they would repeat it for the next shift. Firefighters' children would arrive to have breakfast before school. Many of them were delighted to see their waffles in the shape of Mickey Mouse. The third shift would receive a basket of goodies to enjoy, and every station was given a Mickey Mouse waffle iron.

Visiting schools

As a former teacher, Mayor Spencer has always been especially interested in promoting education, and she has invested her personal money in local schools. She was invited to visit schools for many occasions on a regular basis. Before leaving each school, she would hand a personal check to the principal to use to buy books for the library. She did this so discretely that it was never reported by any news outlet during her three terms as mayor because it was not her intention to gain publicity for the gift. The principals and teachers knew, of course. On several occasions, the principal would ask if her donation could be used to buy other needed items that a tight school budget could not afford.

Countless school and student groups, locally and from abroad, visited Mayor Spencer each year to learn what a mayor does. So many young students were surprised that Huntsville's mayor was a woman. Once at a ribbon-cutting for the Shelby Center at The University of Alabama in Huntsville, Sen. Richard Shelby's granddaughter expressed her surprise that the mayor was a woman.

These groups of students almost always asked an unexpected question or two. By the end of each visit, Mayor Spencer would have talked with them about different parts of the city that they could relate to and would help them to piece together the various parts of the city so they could understood the relationship of the mayor to the city and to the residents.

Mayor Spencer, right, puts on her Cat-in-the-Hat hat along with Susan Anderson, left, and an unknown person for a reading day at Hampton Cove Elementary School.

Supporting the Senior Center

Long before she became mayor of Huntsville, Loretta Spencer was a strong supporter of the Huntsville-Madison County Senior Center. Each year while she was mayor and continuing to the present – with a break during the COVID-19 pandemic – she has sponsored a Huntsville Botanical Garden Galaxy of Lights night out for senior citizens from senior living facilities and high-rises. She provides 14 buses to carry the residents to the garden. The Senior Center coordinates the effort with volunteers and contacts all of the high-rise senior living facilities so as many people as possible can enjoy this festive outing. Most of these individuals would not be able to participate in this beautiful season attraction because many of them don't drive at night or don't have vehicles.

Unusual requests

Occasionally, the public perception of the powers that come with the office of mayor ran counter to the reality. On numerous occasions, engaged couples asked Mayor Spencer if she would perform their marriage ceremony. Of course, she was honored to be asked, but officiating at weddings is not an official or traditional mayoral duty.

"I would have had to get a license," she explains.

Family connections

Mayor Spencer's brother, John Purdy, found out that many people "knew the mayor" but had no clue that he was her brother. They certainly weren't aware that Mayor Spencer and her brother were partners in the family-owned funeral home franchise, Laughlin Service Funeral Home & Crematory. Many times, people would assure John that if he had any trouble arranging for a police escort for funeral processions, they would be glad to contact Mayor Spencer on his behalf because they knew her.

When the city's Operation Green Team wanted a phone number that could be easily remembered, Mayor Spencer thought 53-CLEAN would be memorable and effective. When researching the availability of the number, she was surprised to discover that her daughter, Sarah, and Guy, Sarah's father, had reserved that number as a potential additional business number for The Spencer Companies. She asked Sarah for a favor – to ask her father if they would remove their hold on the number so Operation Green Team could use it. That number is the Litter Hotline used today.

Once, someone asked Mayor Spencer for parenting advice. So many things that she gives to others shows that she exemplifies her response: "Spoil your children, but also teach them to be generous and giving and to notice those that others would not."

From rust to shining silver

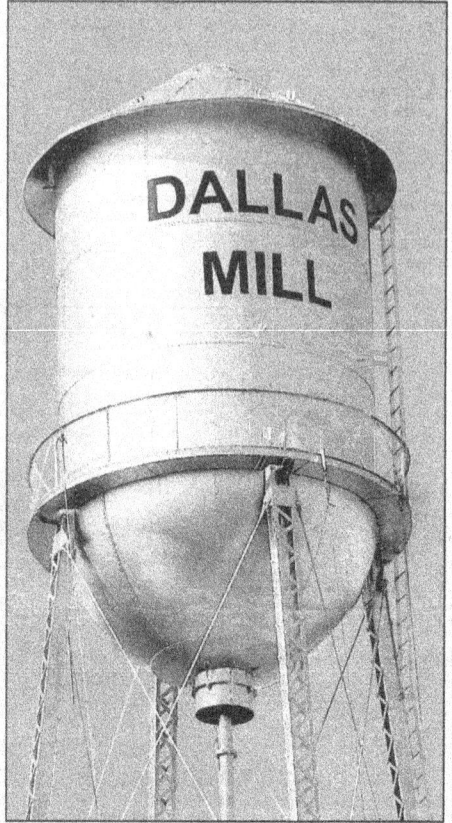

With logos of Dallas Mill on one side and Lincoln Mill on the other, the Dallas Mill water tank is nearing the completion of a $200,000 makeover, right. Six months ago it was a rusty mess, left. All that remains for the project to be complete is attaching steel plates on the legs to prevent anyone from climbing the tank, touching up the paint and landscaping the area. In August 2007, the Huntsville City Council authorized Huntsville Utilities to spend $200,000 to spruce up the rusting tower with a new cone top, reinforced rivets and a coat of silver paint.

Dave Dieter/Huntsville Times

2-26-08

*Mayor Spencer urged the City Council to approve funding
to restore the historic Dallas Mill water tank.
Photo from The Huntsville Times, Feb. 26, 2008.*

Blossomwood Elementary School
1321 Woodmont Avenue
Huntsville, Alabama 35801

Dear Mayor Spencer,

We really appreciate you coming to FAMILY READING NIGHT to read with our children and their parents. Thank you for sharing your love of books with us all.

Sincerely,
Blossomwood Elementary School

Mayor Spencer received this photo and thank-you note after a visit to Blossomwood Elementary School.

Mayor Spencer tries out a locally built "moon buggy"
during a NASA Rover Challenge event.

Chapter Twenty-One:

In Closing — A Personal Note from Loretta Spencer

*T*here are so many more details and experiences that could be added to this memoir. After reading this book of memories, it should be apparent that details and relationships are a vital part of being successful in public office or in any endeavor. It can be difficult to determine which details and relationships should be included and fostered and which ones are not worth the investment of valuable resources. But they all deserve time to be examined. The right details and the right relationships have made the difference in Huntsville's successes.

No person is perfect and no one will get everything right, but having the right people on the team makes the odds of success so much better. And it does take a team to accomplish collective goals — employees, business leaders, corporations, military and, of course, volunteers from all walks of life.

A volunteer learns this quickly. Never discount what you contribute and learn by volunteering.

Huntsville has been fortunate to have so many dedicated members on its team during the years as well as great leadership to help foster new leaders. Leaders who mentored me took time to teach me valuable lessons and be a resource for information and counsel.

I am honored to have been on Huntsville's team for so many years in different roles as a volunteer, a business leader and as your mayor.

Huntsville Police

@HsvPolice

Ms. Spencer just keeps giving back to the city department she loves! She stopped by the South Precinct today with box lunches for all 3 shifts.

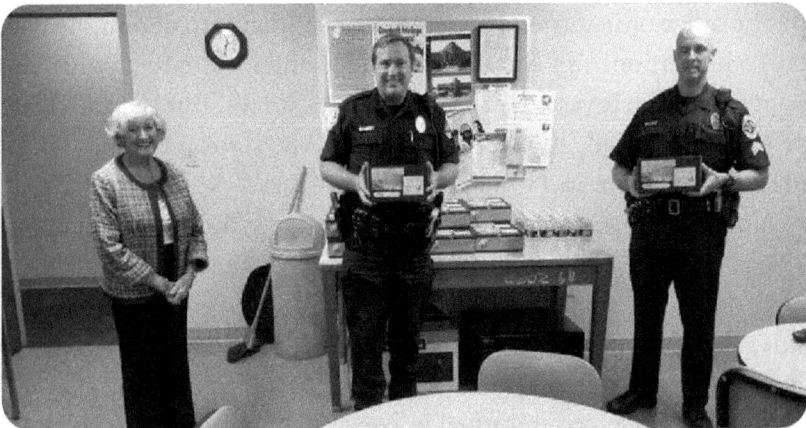

12:40 PM · 28 Apr 20 · Twitter for iPhone

Even after she left office, Loretta Spencer enjoyed showing
her support to city police officers.

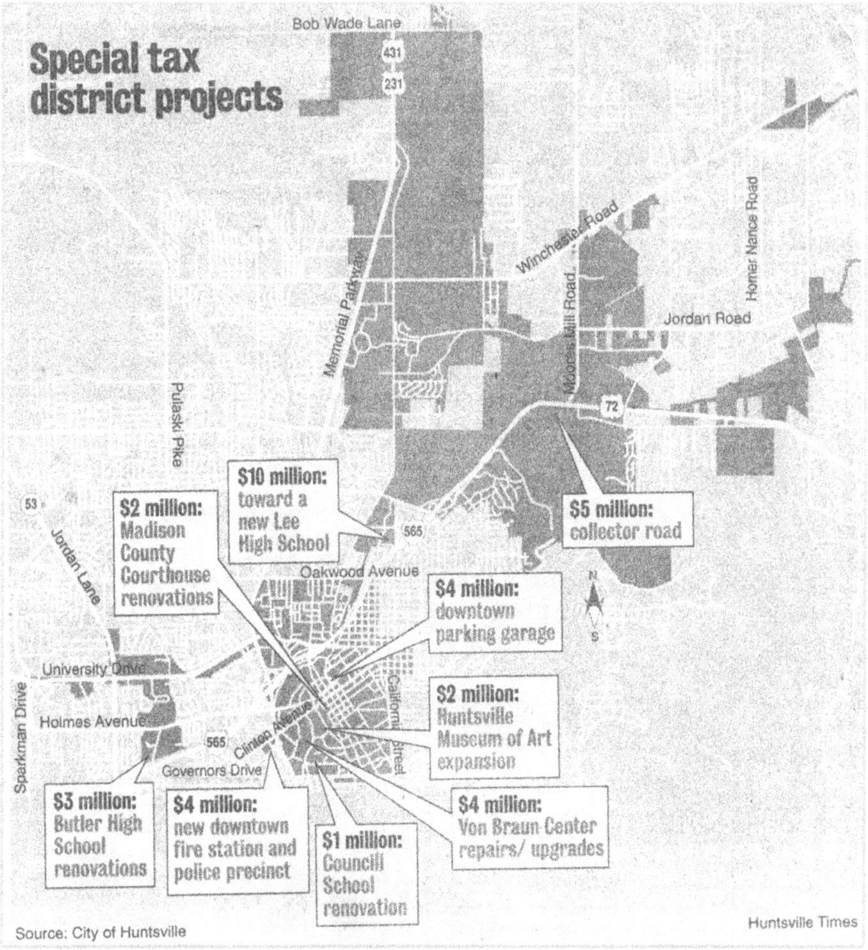

Special tax district projects
Bob Wade Lane
431
231
Winchester Road
Homer Nance Road
Memorial Parkway
Moores Mill Road
Jordan Road
Pulaski Pike
72
$10 million: toward a new Lee High School
$2 million: Madison County Courthouse renovations
$5 million: collector road
53
Jordan Lane
565
Oakwood Avenue
$4 million: downtown parking garage
N
S
University Drive
Sparkman Drive
Holmes Avenue
565
Clinton Avenue
California Street
$2 million: Huntsville Museum of Art expansion
Governors Drive
$3 million: Butler High School renovations
$4 million: new downtown fire station and police precinct
$1 million: Councill School renovation
$4 million: Von Braun Center repairs/ upgrades
Source: City of Huntsville
Huntsville Times

Many of the early financial benefits from Spencer's TIF program, growing and improving existing tax producing properties in Huntsville. The TIFs continued to return additional tax benefits and bonds were paid off ahead of schedule.

Newspaper ad for Loretta Spencer's third term. One of her strengths was delivering on her promises.

Representative Robert "Bud" Cramer at the announcement for the Target distribution center, to be built at Greenbrier Road. Spencer quickly secured additional funding required to win the bid, calling on Alabama Governor Don Siegelman and Rep. Cramer at a critical moment.

Loretta Spencer
HUNTSVILLE'S MAYOR

Let's Get Moving!
Elect Loretta Spencer
Huntsville's Mayor

For over 30 years, **Loretta Spencer** has been
working at the local level to make good things
happen for Huntsville. Now, as **Huntsville's
Mayor, Loretta Spencer** will:

❖ Continue to work for **better education** and
local employment opportunities for our
young people.

❖ Work to make **parental involvement** a
primary part of our schools.

❖ Support the rights of our **senior citizens to
improve their quality of life.**

❖ **Support basic city services like law
enforcement.**

❖ Step-up **business and industry development.**

*A "palm card" from Spencer's first election campaign for Mayor. She won from a total field
of 13 candidates, with many years of service in the community and a broad knowledge
base of city operations.*

The Huntsville Times | Saturday, June 28, 2008

Reaching out to the folks at home

Tourism promoters have issued a brochure encouraging Huntsvillians to tazke what they call a "Stay cation."

City tourism group offers discounts to area attractions

By GINA HANNAH
Times Business Writer
gina.hannah@htimes.com

Huntsville's new tourism campaign is aimed at people who call this area home.

City officials announced a promotion Friday offering discounts to area attractions, hotels and restaurants for the remainder of the summer. The promotion runs Tuesday through Aug. 8, which includes the state's sales-tax-free weekend Aug. 1-3.

Promotional packages include $89 for a dinner for two at Ruth's Chris Steakhouse at the Embassy Suites (regularly well over $100) and 10 percent off weekend room rates at the Westin Huntsville. Area attractions, including the U.S. Space & Rocket Center and Huntsville Botanical Garden, are offering 20 percent off admission.

Judy Ryals, president and CEO of the Huntsville-Madison County Convention & Visitors Bureau, said the goal is to encourage residents to "rediscover Huntsville."

"We have the attractions in our own backyard," she said.

Ryals credited Mayor Loretta Spencer with the idea.

"We have so many attractions here," Spencer said. "We're offering a chance for the public to have fun in Huntsville."

The campaign – spurred in part by skyrocketing gas prices and airfares – will be promoted via radio and newspaper advertisements and billboards, Ryals said.

Some of the discounts can be obtained by printing coupons from www.huntsville.org. For other deals, customers should mention the promotion to the proprietor, she said.

Customers staying in a

Huntsville hotel can win a $1,000 prize package by bringing, mailing or faxing copies of their lodging receipts, Ryals said. A drawing from entries received by Aug. 8 will be held Aug. 15.

Cities around the country have announced "staycation" promotions, encouraging local residents and those living a short drive away to take advantage of nearby attractions during a summer of record gas prices. The Greater Birmingham Con-

vention & Visitors Bureau recently launched its "Your Vacation in Birmingham: A Trip on One Tank," and the Gulf Coast Convention & Visitors Bureau in Mobile has added a "Cruising to the Coast" calculator to its Web site to help calculate gas costs for those planning a drive to the coast.

Last year, Madison County had 2.5 million visitors with an estimated economic impact of $900 million, an increase of 15 percent over the previous year.

With the economy declining nationally, Spencer worked to develop a "Staycation" campaign, urging area residents to experience local attractions and businesses while saving travel expenses.

Revenue collection stirs talk of surplus

Finance chief says city in 'comfortable' spot midway in budget year

By JOHN PECK
Times Staff Writer
john.peck@htimes.com

City revenue is streaming in at an impressive clip, setting the stage for a potentially healthy budget surplus as the mayor and two council members head into the 2008 election season.

City Finance Director Randy Taylor delivered the welcome news Thursday in a midyear budget briefing to the City Council. Overall revenue collected through March was 10.4 percent ahead of the first six months of last year, Taylor reported.

"That puts us in a very comfortable position. It will probably mean we'll have some (more) money to spend," Taylor said at a council work session. The present budget was built on a projected growth of just under 3 percent.

"If that pace continues, we'll have a considerable amount of money available from 2007."

84 The Huntsville Times, Friday, May 11, 2007

Revenue

Continued from page B1

Councilwoman Sandra Moon, chair of the council's finance committee, cautioned that a surplus is not a certainty with several months still remaining in the budget year.

"Even if things look rosy, we want to make sure the money is in the bank before we decide to spend it," she said.

Although budget hearings are still months away, Thursday's budget briefing provided a glimpse of some items that could work their way into the city's 2007-08 spending plan.

Mayor Loretta Spencer asked council members to look for opportunities to buy land for parks whether it be large sites for city recreational fields or smaller tracts for neighborhood parks. Early acquisition would protect open spaces from development and avoid paying higher land prices later. She said the city will work with developers to donate open spaces for parks.

Taylor flagged other potential cost items that could consume some of the budget growth: a cost-of-living adjustment for retired city workers; addition-

Dave Dieter/Huntsville Times

City Finance Director Randy Taylor says sales tax collections are 11.8 percent ahead of the first six months of the last budget year.

al money to complete the beleaguered joint city-county jail (the council previously authorized another $7 million for the $36 million-plus project); several capital expenses including $1 million for major repairs to the Natatorium indoor pool complex; and $500,000 for repairs to the municipal building, city department needs and more money for city employee health and retirement benefits.

Public Works Director Steve

Abbott mentioned outfitting garbage trucks with GPS devices that could track movements and driving speeds. He made that comment after council President Glenn Watson told of seeing a speeding garbage truck.

During the discussion on Natatorium needs, Moon questioned whether it's time to increase admission fees to the pool. Watson bristled, stirring Moon to call for a gradual increase in rates and not a "slam dunk" boost in price.

Councilman Bill Kling expressed hope that the city could recoup some of the rising jail costs through litigation over the previous contracting company the city terminated amid cost overruns and faulty construction.

In his budget report, Taylor said sales tax collections were 11.8 percent ahead of the first six months of last fiscal year. Even if sales taxes and other revenue show little gain over the remaining months, the budget likely will wind up with $6 million or more than projected, he said.

The $66.24 million collected so far in sales taxes surpasses the $55.8 million collected by this time last year. Sales taxes account for nearly 60 percent of the

the $203 million city budget.

How other major revenue sources are faring:

■ Building permits - $4 million projected by year's end, compared with $2.5 million estimated.

■ Privilege license fees – projected to be $1 million more than the $16 million budgeted.

■ TVA in-lieu-of-tax payments – estimated at $3 million, or $400,000 more than budgeted.

■ Interest income from city investments – projected at $3.1 million.

Taylor said expenditures, including fuel expenses, appear to be on track. Taylor cautioned that public safety services face increased demands as the city continues to grow.

He also furnished an analysis of city savings from switching from twice-to once-a-week garbage pickup: $311,729 in personnel costs; $64,193 for fuel (from a base of $505,263); and $363,231 in repairs and maintenance (from a base of $1.16 million).

The figures compare fiscal 2005 with fiscal 2006 when the reduced collection schedule went into effect.

City Finance Director Randy Taylor helped Spencer and the city grow Huntsville and create new revenue for public needs. Never one to pursue the spotlight, he was an invaluable asset to Huntsville.

While space and missile defense work is common to many in Huntsville, Spencer regularly pursued opportunities that benefit the industry and Huntsville in general. Loretta saw the value in participating in meetings and showing local support.

Fortune 500 companies garner the majority of attention in the local business community, but Spencer regularly recognized small businesses and their growth. She is shown here at a ribbon cutting of a new Domino's Pizza serving the growing Hampton Cove area in the late 1990s.

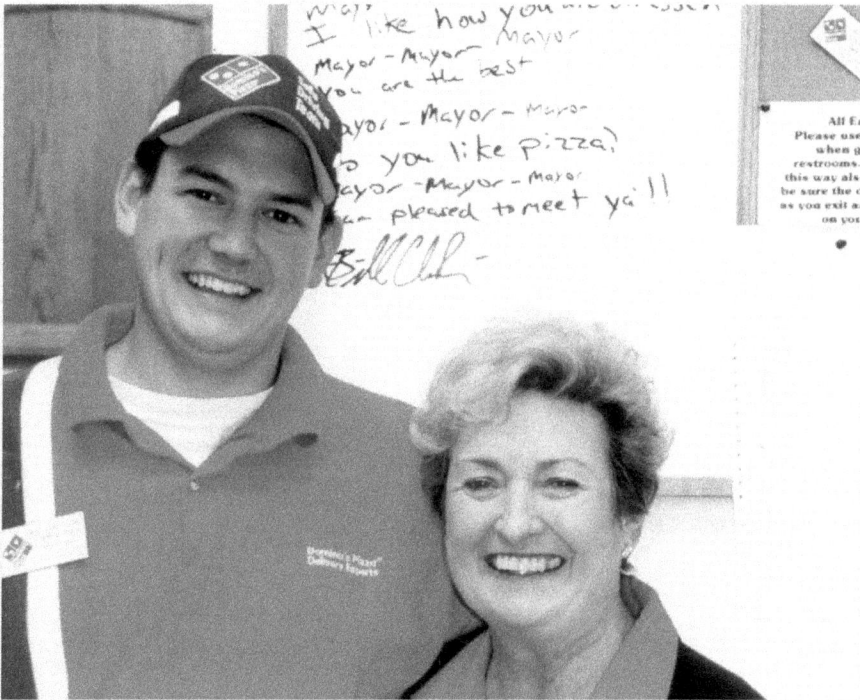

Always one to warmly welcome and greet people, Spencer appreciates this Domino's employee's poem to honor her attending the ribbon-cutting that he posted on the board behind them.

About Loretta Spencer

$\mathcal{A}$ supportive spouse and involved parent, Loretta Spencer continued her lifelong passion for service by acting as a community volunteer and leading as the first female mayor of Huntsville, Alabama. Loretta took on many challenges, bringing together people to achieve the goals of individuals, businesses, and the city. She brought decades of diverse experience to the job, achieving great success for the people. *In Loretta Spencer: A Passion for Service*, she tells the stories and shares her secrets for helping Huntsville grow into Alabama's biggest city. She continues to support local causes, providing her unique experience and knowledge.

Fresh Ink Group

Independent Multi-media Publisher

Fresh Ink Group / Push Pull Press
Voice of Indie / GeezWriter

❦

Hardcovers
Softcovers
All Ebook Formats
Audiobooks
Podcasts
Worldwide Distribution

❦

Indie Author Services
Book Development, Editing, Proofing
Graphic/Cover Design
Video/Trailer Production
Website Creation
Social Media Marketing
Writing Contests
Writers' Blogs

❦

Authors
Editors
Artists
Experts
Professionals

❦

FreshInkGroup.com
info@FreshInkGroup.com
X: @FreshInkGroup
Facebook.com/FreshInkGroup
LinkedIn: Fresh Ink Group
Instagram: @FreshInkGroup and @FIGPublishing

Fresh Ink Group
FreshInkGroup.com

www.ingramcontent.com/pod-product-compliance
Lightning Source LLC
Chambersburg PA
CBHW052056090426
42739CB00010B/2208